A Guide to Our Two Savannahs

Ellis Garvin

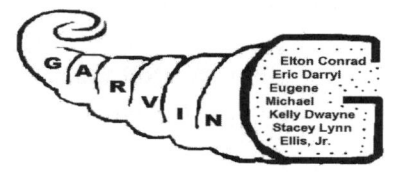

Garvin Publishing Company
2302 Lincoln Street
Savannah, Georgia 31401

Many people book tours with tour companies and do not see what they intended or wanted to see. This guide and a small effort on the part of the tourist seeking a tour of Savannah will eliminate this problem.

All rights reserved. This publication may not be copied or reproduced in whole or part without the express written consent of the author.

Photography by Ellis Garvin

Cover Photos clockwise from top left: Cotton Exchange Building, Prince Hall, Yamacraw Village Sign, The Landing Sign, Laural Grove Cemetery, South Laural Grove Cemetery, Unknown Confederate Soldiers, Unknown Slaves. The three black and white shots, Marcus Garvey, Martin Luther King Jr., Restaurant with separate Black and White entrances are from another source.

ISBN: 978-0-9824649-0-8

Copyright © 2009, 2010
by Ellis Garvin

Table of Contents

Acknowledgements / 5

Introduction / 7

A Driving Tour of Savannah / 9

Savannah's Beautiful Squares / 103

Must See Places / 129

Questions and Answers about Savannah / 147

Bibliography / 153

Index / 155

Acknowledgments

Many people have helped to make this guide possible: family members, friends, strangers, and anyone who would allow me to question them. In fact, my favorite daughter is angry with me because of this guide. A list of helpers would exceed the length of the guide itself, so to all my helpers I extend my heart felt appreciation and thanks.

Introduction

SAVANNAH HAS MANY GUIDED tours available to visitors. Only one of them, however— this one—includes more than one or two sites relating to that half of the city's population (the African-American half) whose energy, labor, and imaginations underlay so many of the achievements of the other, more visible half, the white half.

As a result the real story of how Savannah got built too often remains untold. African-American Tours will remedy this neglect. It is our belief that visitors deserve better and want better. They want the truth, a truth that is far more vital and intriguing than any scrubbed up, lesser version could ever be.

Many of the very bricks used to build the fine old buildings in the downtown historic district, for instance, were made by the slaves at Hermitage Plantation. It took the slaves one full year to get the columns up the cliffs from River Street and in place to form the front of the United States Custom House on Bay Street.

Even freed African-Americans had to donate two or three days each month to work on public projects, such as the ramps up from River Street to Bay Street and the walls that keep Bay Street from falling down onto River Street. African-Americans paid more taxes than non-African-Americans in Savannah. When these things are said, many people say, "That's African-American history!" I beg to differ. This is Savannah's history! I repeat. This is Savannah's history!

This history should be told, not to offend or blame but to inform and enlighten. You will find it in this book.

A Guide to Our Two Savannahs

Start: Visitors Center Parking Lot

WELCOME TO SAVANNAH! My name is Ellis Garvin, the author of this book and your guide. To understand Savannah you must think of it as two cities.

For example, when I was a boy, the building directly in front of you was the Central of Georgia Railroad Station, designed by architect Alfred Eichberg. It was owned by the Central of Georgia Railroad. There was a sign over one door that said, "COLORED," and one over the other door that said, "WHITE."

My father worked for the Seaboard Coastline Railroad, and Union Station was a stone's throw south of this location. My family and I were in and out of Union Station quite often, because we had relatives that lived in Savannah. We rode the train on employee passes, and when the train filled up we had to move to the back and give up our free seats to the paying passengers.

The Savannah History Museum and Visitors Center

However, if the train filled up with white passengers, other black passengers—even paying passengers—had to give up their seats and move to the back of the train along with us.

Now, that has all changed! We pay for a ticket and keep our seat for the whole trip.

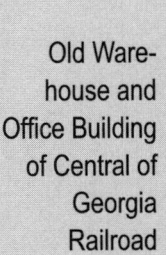

Old Warehouse and Office Building of Central of Georgia Railroad

The buildings shown above were once owned by the Central of Georgia Railroad; they are now owned by Savannah College of Art and Design. SCAD came to Savannah in 1978, and they have been good for Savannah. They replaced years of decay and neglect with renovation and fresh paint. The buildings shown here were constructed with Savannah grey bricks. These bricks were made by the slaves at Hermitage Plantation, several miles west of the city on the Savannah River. They were cheap. Many builders added a coat of stucco over these bricks to hide them.

Times have changed. Recently someone stole three hundred of these bricks from another location. The lowest estimate for the value of the stolen bricks was five thousand dollars. That would make each brick that you see in these buildings worth over sixteen dollars. The reason for the steep price is that when Hermitage Plantation closed down and slavery ended, no one kept the formula for making Savannah Grey Bricks. Today they are collectables.

If you hear someone mention "The back to Africa movement," one of the first names you might think of would be that of Marcus Garvey. Marcus Garvey was an excellent speaker, a great organizer, and at one time he had over two million followers.

Right onto Fahm St.

Garvey accepted money from many people including the Ku Klux Klan. He bought three ships and started the Black Star Steam Ship Line; however, Marcus Garvey never helped one African-American get back to Africa, nor did he ever visit Africa himself.

Right onto Turner Blvd.

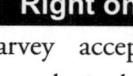

Marcus Garvey

On your left is a monument to Bishop Henry McNeal Turner. He was the first African-American to be made chaplain in the Union Army. He was appointed to this position by President Abraham Lincoln. He sponsored two ships returning to Africa. When the first of these ships left Savannah there was not much fanfare.

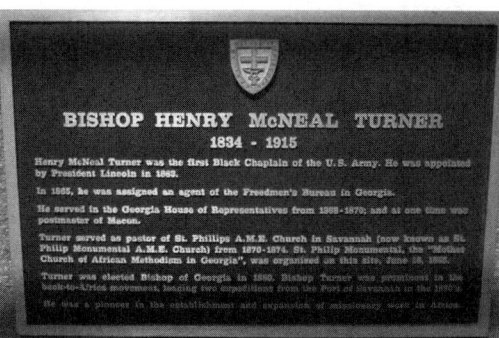

Bishop Henry McNeal Turner Monument

Left onto Papy Street

But the second ship was sent on its way with an attendance of church choirs, bands, singing, and a the cheers of a throng of people, black and white, who had come out to see the Africans off to Africa. The City Council noticed all this enthusiasm and passed a law requiring each African-American leaving Savannah going back to Africa to pay a fee of two hundred dollars. Well, that was the end of the "Back to Africa Movement" for Savannah because most African-Americans in the city were unable to come up with the additional two hundred dollars, plus the fare for their passage.

The Back to Africa Movement helped not more than two hundred African-Americans from Savannah get back to Africa from 1820 to 1896.

General James Edwards Oglethorpe's Monument in Chippewa Square

When General Oglethorpe came to Georgia in 1733, the Trustees of the colony had four prohibitions:
1. Beer, wine and ale were allowed, but rum and brandy wre prohibited. The settlers broke this prohibition almost immediately.

2. No Lawyers were allowed. If you had to appear in court, you could speak for yourself or a friend could speak for you. You know this prohibition was broken because today Georgia has just as many lawyers per capita as any other state in the Union.
3. No black slaves or Negroes were allowed. This prohibition was broken before General Oglethorpe arrived in the colony. Black slaves were used to survey and to do the heavy work of clearing the land.
4. No Papists or Catholics could worship in the colony of Georgia. The reason for this was that the Catholics or Papists spoke Spanish and the Spanish controlled Florida at the time. The colonists thought that the Catholics would be loyal to the Spaniards and thus pose a danger to the colony. Today, Savannah has one the most beautiful Catholic churches in all of North American, Saint John the Baptist Cathedral, and if you get the chance, go see it. It is on Abercorn and East Charlton Streets on Layette Square.

Left onto West Bryan Street

Yamacraw Village

As we turn onto West Bryan, we are entering into Yamacraw Village. The name comes from the Yamacraw Indians that lived here at the time of General Oglethorpe's arrival in 1733.

Yamacraw Village is one of the oldest public housing projects in all of North America, and as you look to your left you will see the boarded up windows and decay typical of much public housing throughout our country.

Yamacraw Village Square

Yamacraw Village Square is the only square in Savannah that I am positive that the slavers did not sell slaves in, and that is because this square has only been open since 2006. It was built to recognize the contributions that the Indians and African-Americans made to the colony of Georgia. The Yamacraw Indians are credited with being the first to make pottery in North America. The three sculptures in the square were done by Jerome Meadows, an African-American sculptor.

Bryan's Historical Marker

In 1788, at Brampton's barn, the Ethiopian Church of Jesus Christ was established by sixty-seven members. Later, Rev. Andrew Bryan would be ordained a minister there, and the church would become the first African-American Baptist Church in the United States of America. Rev. Bryan would later buy his own freedom for one hundred pounds sterling.

First Bryan Baptist Church

Across the street is First Bryan Baptist Church, and it sits on the oldest piece of property owned continuously by African-Americans in all of North America. Above the door is a picture of Rev. Andrew Bryan, who bought the property for fifty pounds sterling. The monument on the right on the right of the entrance is in honor of Rev. George Leile, the first African-American Baptist Missionary in North America. I will tell you more about him later.

Right onto Fahm Street

If you look ahead and slightly to the left you will see the Talmadge Memorial Bridge; it is just under a mile and a half long; it has a clearance of one hundred and eighty-five feet at high tide; it is made up of sixty-two 30 by 80 segments of concrete roadbed each weighting 300 tons. This bridge spans the Savannah River, joining South Carolina to downtown Savannah.

Above, the Talmadge Bridge. Below, a container ship enters the Savannah port

The height of this bridge allows the Savannah port to potentially handle 98 percent of all the ships in the world, making the Port of Savannah one of the largest container ports on the East coast.

Right onto Bay Street

The bridge was named after Herman Talmadge, one of Georgia's worst Governors for black people. In 1946, when Herman Talmadge was running for the office of governor, a reporter reported: "The dead arose from their graves and marched in alphabetical order to the polls, cast their ballots and returned to their repose." Within a month after Herman Talmadge had taken office four African-Americans had been lynched in Georgia. To this day, no arrests have been made nor have any indictments been returned for those atrocities.

We have been taught to believe Georgia was a "debtors colony." This idea is more myth than fact. When Oglethorpe arrived in Georgia in 1733, there were 114 settlers on the ship Anne. Of these, less than one third were debtors. Earlier in his life, General Oglethorpe had a friend who wrote a book and borrowed money to publish it. The book did not sell well, so he was unable to repay his debts. He went to jail, and while there he contracted smallpox and died. This tragic event made Oglethorpe want to do something to help England's debtors. When the idea came up to start a colony for debtors, Oglethorpe was all for it. This altruistic idea was used to raise money to establish the colony of Georgia, but the real reasons for doing so were to create a buffer zone for the colony of South Carolina against the threat of the Spaniards in Florida; to provide a new source of raw materials for English factories; to create a new market for England's manufactured goods; and to provide a cheap source of silk.

Left onto MLK Boulevard

The Savannah River at the North End of MLK Blvd.

On December 17, 1864, General Sherman sent a letter to the Confederate forces garrisoned in Savannah demanding the surrender of the city. Sherman and his officers awaited the answer to his ultimatum. Meanwhile, the Confederate Forces built a pontoon bridge across the Savannah River at the foot of MLK Boulevard and escaped into South Carolina. After The Confederate soldiers had escaped, Mayor Richard Arnold surrendered the City of Savannah to General Geary. General Sherman was in Richmond Hill in an unsuccessful attempt to cut off the escape of the Confederate forces.

Right onto River Street

On the right you will see the barracoons. They will look like a garage without a door; there are four of them, but you will be able to see only two. This is where the slaves were kept before going into one of the squares to be sold. These holding pens did not need any doors because the slaves where held in shackles and chains, and the chains could be attached to any stationary object. Thus the slaves would be tethered like a dog, cow, or any other animal. At Tybee Island, ten miles East of Savannah, there was a 104-acre tract that made up a lazaretto—a kind of holding pen—and this is where the slaves first entered Georgia from Africa or other places. There, they would be checked for diseases, and fattened up if necessary. When the slaves reached the barracoons, they would be ready for market.

The Barracoons, or slave holding cells

On the left is the African-American monument. It has a man, a woman, a boy, and a girl with broken chains at their feet, symbolizing the end of slavery. At the base of the monument is an inscription by Maya Angelou, "We were stolen, sold and brought together from the African continent. We got on the slave ships together. We lay back to belly in the holds of the slave

The African-American monument

ships in each others excrement and urine together, sometimes died together, and our lifeless bodies thrown overboard together. Today, we are standing up together, with faith and even some joy." Savannah has many monuments, yet this is only the second monument erected in Savannah for African-Americans. To get this project off the ground, Dr. Abigail Jordan, a former teacher of Savannah State University, had to put up one hundred thousands dollars of her own money.

Across the river is Hutchinson Island. When I was a boy, I was told Daddy Grace was from there. I will tell you more about Daddy Grace later.

Before coming back to this area in 1976, I had seen in travel magazines Cap'N Sam, and Cap' N Sam's name was spelled C-A-P' N Sam. The "tai" was left out of the word, just the way we Southerners would say it.

Cap'n Sam was as dark as we African-Americans come; he had on a white uniform, a white cap, and epaulets on his shoulders. I was on River Street one day, and saw Cap'n Sam standing there on the sidewalk. He spoke to me, and I just stood there dumfounded. I had thought that he was a model or some computer-generated image. Never did I think he was a real person, and until this day I have not returned his greeting. Cap'n Sam owned the excursion boats tied up at the dock and ran a ferry service to Hilton Head and Duafuskie Islands. He was the only African-American who owned property on River Street

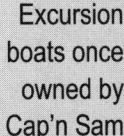

Excursion boats once owned by Cap'n Sam

The rough stones that we walk on on River Street are cobblestones; they are uniform because they were cut at a quarry for paving. The stones that are irregular are ballast stones; they get their name from what they were used for, to give a ship ballast in rough weather. Many ships coming from England were mostly empty, and these stones were used to stabilize the them.

Cobble stones (l) on River Street. Balast stones (r) on the embankment

If you will look to your right, you will see a bridge or walkway because the Cotton Exchange was the first building in Savannah to utilize air space. I will tell you more about it when we get back up on Bay Street.

This walkway is Savannah's first use of airspace.

Across the river is the Savannah International Trade & Convention Center, and it happens to be one of the few buildings in Savannah that dons the modern style of architecture; the building on the right of the Convention Center is the Westin Hotel, and it has an eighteen-hole golf course designed by Robert Cupp and Sam Snead.

The Savannah Convention Center

On your left, you will find hucksters with their over-priced wares. Most of the things they are selling are not even made here.

The River Street Mall

A Guide to Our Two Savannahs

The Waving Girl

The Waving Girl, Florence Martus, was nineteen in 1887 when she began to wave a greeting to the ships entering and leaving the Port of Savannah, with her apron during the day and a lantern at night. This continued for the next forty-four years.

Florence Martus did not do her waving here on River Street but on Elba Island at the mouth of the Savannah River, where she lived with her father and her brother, who was the lighthouse keeper on Cockspur Island. It was rumored that Florence fell in love with a seaman who never returned to accept her love. There are some who believe she was the most loyal woman of our time, and there are others who think that she was the biggest fool of our time. Now that you have the facts, you make the call.

Next, there is the Olympic cauldron, which represents the yachting events held at Tybee Island in 1996.

The Olympic Cauldron

Up the Ramp to Bay Street

On the right is the Old Harbor Light. It was put there in1852 to warn other ships of those that the British had sunk in the harbor. As you can see, it is of little use today because of the trees that have grown up all around it.

Old Harbor Light

Also on the right, your see the Vietnam Memorial. The monument was built in the shape of Vietnam, and all the names of the soldiers from this area who lost their lives in that war are engraved in the white marble of the monument.

Vietnam Monument

On the right is Savannah's Irish and Robert Emmet Park. The Irish Monument is dedicated to all past, present and future Irish. The Salzburger Monument and Park is the next attraction on the right. The Salzburgers, settlers of German heritage, came to Savannah in 1734 and settled at Ebenezer.

Irish Monument in Emmet Park on Bay Street

Left onto Lincoln Street

Presently, we are in one of the most expensive areas in Savannah. A building in this area can cost a million dollars and more.

Right onto President Street

The yellow building on our right is the old stables and slave quarters of the Owen-Thomas House.

The next building on our right is the Owen-Thomas House. Many feel it is the finest example of Regency Architecture in all of North America. It was designed by William Jay. In 1825, the Marquis de Lafayette was a guest here. He addressed the people of Savannah from the side balcony.

Right onto Abercorn Street

Old Stables and Slave Quarters of the Owen-Thomas House.

The Owen-Thomas House.

On our left is Oglethorpe Square, named for General James Edward Oglethorpe, founder of the Colony of Georgia. The next square is Reynolds Square, and it was named for the first Royal Governor of Georgia. The monument in this square is that of the Reverend John Wesley, erected by the Methodists of Georgia in honor of their founder.

Left onto Bay Street

A Guide to Our Two Savannahs

Savannah Cotton Exchange

The Cotton Exchange is the first building in Savannah to incorporate airspace. The cotton factors needed dock space on River Street and office space on Bay Street. The ramps needed to remain open to allow the wagons to bring the cotton and other raw materials down to the dock to be loaded onto the ships.

In 1793, cotton was on the decline as a money crop in Georgia as well as all over the South. Then Eli Whitney and his friend Miller were visiting the Mulberry Plantation. Whitney saw the difficulty the slaves had separating the seeds from the cotton, and developed a technique for doing so, the first cotton gin. Whitney and Miller thought that the invention would make them rich, but the invention was so simple that most people just made one for themselves.

The red brick building on the right is the cotton exchange, and all the buildings in this group are called "Factors Walk." Soon after the invention of the cotton gin cotton became king, and the price of cotton was decided right there in the Cotton Exchange. The Exchange and the mythological griffin, a monster that is a cross between a lion and an eagle, was designed by William Preston.

Remember the two Savannahs: the cotton exchange is now the Free Masons meeting hall for the white Masonic members

George and Martha

In 1791, President George Washington stopped in Savannah. He was received so well by the distinguished citizens of the city that on his returned to Washington he sent the two cannons that you see on the right as a token of his gratitude. The cannons were captured at Yorktown by the local militia, the Chatham Artillery. One is English and the other is French. The French cannon has King Louis XIV's inscription in Latin: "The Last Resort of Kings." Because of their opposite shapes, the guns have been referred to as "George and Martha."

On your left is the Custom House; the first steel and fireproof building built in Savannah. It has steel doors that can be closed, making the building a veritable fortress. It was designed by John Norris in 1846.

In 1889, Col. John DeVeaux was appointed the chief collection agent by President William McKinley. Col. DeVeaux was the first African-American to hold that position in all of North America, and he held it until his death in 1909. It took slaves an entire year to move the six columns from the docks on River Street up to Bay Street and put them in place. They did it all with rollers, rope, and their own muscles as tools.

United States Custom House

City Hall

On the right is City Hall, and it was designed by Hyman Witcover in 1905. The building's fancy exterior was left off due to the lack of financial resources. The interior presents an air of opulence with its circular balconies and stained glass dome. The gold used to cover the dome was the gift of a local philanthropist. The use of gold to cover the dome is in recognition of Savannah's being the Capital of Georgia from 1782 to 1785.

Bench marking Oglethorpe's tent site

On the right is a white marble bench where General Oglethorpe is said to have pitched his first tent on arrival in the colony of Georgia.

Renovation of Ellis Square

On the left, now being rebuilt, is Ellis Square. The square was named after Georgia's second Royal Governor. The city is in the process of building an underground garage on the site and restoring Ellis Square on the surface. When I was a boy, I remember coming into this area to sell the things that we grew on our farm— squash, beans, peas, okra, and whatever else we had to sell—because this was the location of the farmer's market. On occasion, I remember my father not liking the prices we were offered for our produce, so we would take it into Yamacraw Village and into another neighborhood called Frog Town and peddle what we had in the streets. What we did not sell, we would take back home and feed it to the farm animals.

Bay Street, the Street we are on now, was once called North Broad, and it was the North boundary of Savannah.

Left onto Montgomery Street

Here you find Franklin Square; it was named after Benjamin Franklin. This square was once known as Water Tower or Reservoir Square. More on the square in a later section of this book.

A Guide to Our Two Savannahs

The Haitian monument

The Haitian American Historical Society with the City of Savannah has put up a monument in honor of the Haitians, who fought on the side of the colonists in the Siege of Savannah in 1779. I do not know how this monument will honor the Haitian people, because they did not get their own freedom until 1883. Why fight for someone else's freedom before you obtain your own freedom?

The story of the Haitians volunteering to come to American and fight on the side of the colonists makes for good press, but a more logical reason and maybe nearer to the truth is that the French, who were in charge of Haiti in 1779, brought several hundred Haitians to Savannah to aid the colonists in their efforts. This was in the best interests of the France and not of the Haitian people.

Right onto West Bryan Steet

The First African Baptist Church was built in 1859 by African-Americans for African-Americans. This project was started under the leadership of Reverend Andrew Marshall, who passed away three years before it was completed. Slaves made the bricks for this church at the Savannah River. The women brought the bricks up from the river in their aprons. Much of this work was

First African Baptist Church

done by the slaves after they had put in a full day's work on the plantation where they lived. First African Baptist Church was the first brick church built in North America for African-Americans.

The ceiling inside the First African Baptist Church

The ceiling in the church has nine-motif pattern panels. This was a way of letting run-away slaves and others to know that this building was a safe house.

Stained glass windows behind the altar

Behind the Altar are the stained glass windows showing six of the first seven ministers of first African Baptist Church. On the right: Andrew Bryan, Andrew Cox Marshall, and William Campbell. On the left: George Gibbons, Emmanuel King Love, and James Carr. The first Minister of this congregation was Reverend George Leile, who started it at Brampton Plantation in 1788. Reverend Leile's portrait is on a stained glass window on the front of the church. The original pews in the balcony of First African Baptist Church were built by slaves. The markings on the sides of each pew tell of the builder and where he came from. The slave builders spoke different languages, so the markings on each pew are different.

The holes in the floor on the first floor, forming the shape of a diamond, are called Kongo Cosmograms or Yowa. They had two functions: One, they represented the signs of the cosmos and the continuity of human life. Two, they allowed the run-

One of the Original Pews in the Balcony of First African Baptist Church

away slaves hiding under the floor to breathe.

The First African Baptist Church was a stop on the Underground Railroad. Under this floor there was another floor four feet lower. This cavity allowed run-away slaves to hide during the day. There were tunnels leading out to the Savannah River. At the river the slaves would look to catch a ship going north to freedom.

A Kongo cosmogram

A Guide to Our Two Savannahs

The Gopherwood Pulpit

The gopher wood pulpit is on the first floor of First African Baptist Church along with the Kongo Cosmograms are mysteries of First African Baptist. Gopher wood is not found in this country.

Where is the entrance to the tunnels leading to the Savannah River? Or how could the African-Americans build this church under such adverse conditions? These are mysteries that the First African Baptist Church refuses to give up. This church is a must see for all interested in the struggles of African-Americans during slavery.

The boarded up red brick building on the right was one of Savannah's largest slave markets. It was owned by a Mr. Joseph Bryan. This was not the only place that slaves were sold! They sold slaves in almost all the squares in Savannah. Wright Square was the most popular because the courthouse was there. A platform would be erected in front of the courthouse to display the slaves to be sold, and they punished slaves in the squares to intimidate the other slaves. Mr. Bryan conducted the auctioning of

The slave market of Joseph Bryan

the 436 slaves for Pierce Butler who had to sell his slaves to pay off gambling debts incurred here in Savannah, at the Savannah Racetrack in 1857. The location of the racetrack would be in the vicinity of Lily Street and Augusta Road on the Westside.

Left onto MLK Bouldevard

MLK Boulevard was once West Broad Street, and it was the West boundary of Savannah and as we reach the other two boundaries, I will point them out. MLK was the First Street to be paved in Savannah, because in rainy weather the wagons bringing in cotton, rice, and other freight would get bogged down on their way to the Savannah River.

The yellow building on the right is the Scarborough House, designed by William Jay and built for William Scarborough, one of the backers of the first steam ship to cross the Atlantic Ocean, the "S. S. Savannah." This building was known as the West Side School. It was the first effort Savannah made to educate African-

A Guide to Our Two Savannahs

The Scarborough House

Americans. A man named George DeRenne, a planter, put up the money to buy the building. It is now the Ships of the Sea Museum.

Remember the two Savannahs? At the traffic light is Broughton Street, and this is where the whites did their shopping. West Broad street, now Martin Luther King Boulevard, is where the African-Americans did their shopping. During the 1960s, Levy's department store and McCory's Lunch counter on Broughton Street were where the sit-ins took place. The marchers had a sign that read, "We can buy a fifty dollar suit, but we can't buy a ten cent cup of coffee." Hosea Williams led some of the sit-ins.

The Chatham County courthouse

The building on our left is our Court House, and the next

The Chatham County Jail is our jail. These two buildings are sitting where Liberty Square once was. It was named for the Liberty Boys, those who wanted to break away from England, and the Liberty Flame burns on the other side of the Court House.

Savannah Civic Center

Across the Street is the Civic Center, and sits where Elbert Square once was. Elbert Square was named after a planter, and he was a Liberty boy too. When General Oglethorpe arrived in Georgia, he had the plans all laid out for Savannah. These plans included twenty-four squares, and Liberty and Eldert are the two lost squares.

The next traffic light marks Oglethorpe Avenue. It was once called South Broad, and was the South boundary of the city.

A Guide to Our Two Savannahs

The old Central of Georgia Station

When I was boy, West Broad (now MLK) was the busiest Street in Savannah because on the right was the old Central of Georgia Station (now the Visitor's Center). Trains were arriving and departing around the clock day and night here and at Union Station down the street, so the lights would be on all night.

Battlefield, Savannah Heritage Park

On the right is Battlefield Park. This is where the Siege of Savannah took place in 1779 and where the Haitains fought on the side of the colonists against the British. The British used several hundred African-Americans to help build that fortification on the right, and they armed two hundred more to fight against the colonists. In this battle, Africans fought against Africans. The Haitians were from Africa and so were the African-American slaves. In 1782, the British left Savannah with thirty-five hundred African-Americans. In that group was Rev. George Liele, the first African-American missionary Baptist preacher in North America. He preached at the plantations on the Savannah River, and he baptized Rev. Andrew Bryan at Brampton Plantation. He left Savannah with the British, and he started the first Baptist Church in Jamaica.

The Roundhouse Railroad Museum

On the right and south of the Battlefield is the Roundhouse Railroad Museum. The museum has a roundhouse and repair shop, one of the few that are still operational in the United States. Train enthusiasts should not miss this one.

Before and during the 60's, there were stores on both sides of this street owned and operated by African-Americans: grocery stores, hardware stores

To the left and top right: ruins of African-American businesses of yesteryear.

barber shops, banks, beauty salons, funeral parlors, fish markets, and a pharmacy. Now, many people ask, "What happen to all the businesses owned by African-Americans?"

Well! The Interstate and urban renewal did their share of destroying African-American businesses, but integration was the big culprit. Blacks began to leave the neighborhood and shop in the white stores, neglecting their own stores. As a result, many of our own stores had to close because of a lack of customers.

The Civil Rights Museum

On the left is the Civil Rights Museum, named after Ralph Mark Gilbert, who revitalized the NAACP in Savannah and became its president. At the same time, he was the Minister to First African Baptist Church.

Bynes-Royall Funeral Home

On the right, about where Wendy's is sitting, once sat the oldest continuously owned African-American business in Savannah: Bynes & Royall Funeral Home. When Mr. Bynes had to move his business to make room for the I-16 overpass, the City gave him twenty-six thousand dollars. Some years later, Wendy's bought the same property from the city for over two million dollars.

Site of the Dunbar Theater and Dunbar Hotel

The Dunbar Theater, built in 1935, once sat over where the chicken place now stands. Above was the Dunbar hotel. This is where the big acts like Cab Callaway would perform and stay upstairs in the hotel when in Savannah.

The Star Theater stood on this site

On the left in the vacant lot is where the Star Theater was located. It was built in 1931, and it was the first theater in Savannah owned by blacks.

On the right is St. Phillip Monumental A.M.E., Georgia's oldest African Methodist Episcopal congregation. It was founded in 1865, and this is where Bishop Henry McNeal Turner was the Pastor when he was in Savannah.

St. Phillip AME Church

Carver State Bank

Next to the church is Carver State Bank, the only bank in Savannah still owned and operated by African-Americans. Would you believe that one time right here on MLK or West Broad there were four banks owned and operated by African-Americans? One bank, Wage Earners Bank, operated out of the same building that the Civil Rights Museum is in now, and should you ever go there you can still see the old bank's safe.

Savannah Pharmacy

Coming up on the left is the second oldest continuously owned African-American business in Savannah, Savannah Pharmacy. At one time, Savannah Pharmacy had three other locations, but recently in an interview, Mr. Fonvielle said that they are all closed, and he is barely making ends meet with this last store. In 2007 Savannah Pharmacy closed its doors.

Frazier Homes

On the right is Frazier Homes, and some of you younger people who listen to hip hop music may have heard of a group called Outkast. Well, one of its members, Big Boi, lived in this project, but he did not become famous while living here. He moved to Atlanta before becoming famous. He was in Savannah recently, and he had an event called "Ball 2 you Fall."

Right onto Anderson Street

St. Matthew Episcopal Church

The church across the Street on the corner is St. Matthew

Episcopal Church; this church was formed when St. Stephens from the East side, where the lighter skin African-Americans attended and St. Augustine from Yamacraw Village where the darker skin African-Americans attended, were combined. When they first came together, the lighter skin African-Americans sat on one side, and the darker skin African-Americans sat on the other side. Now! Before you indict Savannah, understand that this happened in Atlanta, Charleston, New Orleans, and many other cities where there were former slaves.

Cuyler Street School

first public school for Blacks

The red brick building on the right is the first school built from the ground up by the Savannah Board of Education to educate African-Americans in Savannah. It was built in 1913.

Left onto Ogeeche Road

On the Right is Laurel Grove Cemetery. The section that you see here is North Laurel Grove and this is where the Whites are buried. Remember the two Savannahs; the Blacks are buried in what is called South Laurel Grove.

There was a man named George Stiles, and he owned a slave named Black Frank. These two were inseparable as children; they both grew up and became musicians; they both went into the Confederate Army and still were inseparable; they came out of the army and remained inseparable. When George died, he was laid to rest in North Laurel Grove; some years later, Black Frank died, and he was laid to rest in South Laurel Grove. Now the strange thing about George and Frank, these two would not allow slavery or a civil war to separate them, but the moment they died, Savannah had no difficulty in parting these life-long friends.

Laurel Grove Cemetery

United House of Prayer for All People

On the right is one of Daddy Grace's Churches. I know of at lease two others that are in Savannah. This one has a cafeteria in the back. I have been told that they serve good food.

I-16 off and on ramp

Before I-16 came into Savannah, there was no physical line of demarcation to separate North Laurel Grove from South Laurel Grove; however, the line was well known because there are no Blacks buried in North Laurel Grove, and there are no Whites buried in South Laurel Grove, even until today.

Right onto 37th Street

Two houses on 37th Street

You do not need to be told that this is not the choicest section of Savannah, but do not think that these houses are worthless. I came back to this area in 1976; I bought a one bath, three-bedroom house for twenty-five thousand dollars. Today, the same house is worth about two hundred fifty thousand dollars. So, any house in the downtown area of Savannah is probably worth more than you would think.

Entrance, South Laurel Grove Cemetery

Entering South Laurel Grove, where African-Americans are buried, look at the top of the historical marker on the left, at the top of the circle: "Non Sibi Sed Aliis." Please see that because it is important, and I will explain it later.

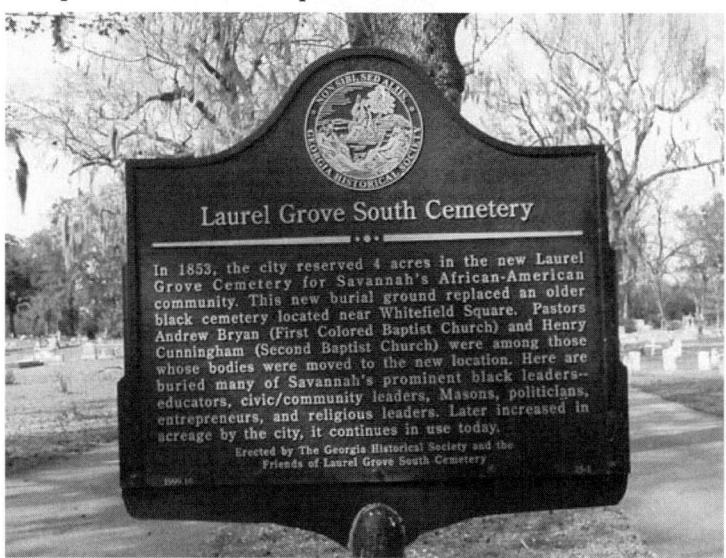

Laurel Grove South Cemetery historical marker

Mr. W.W. Law was the first person to start a tour in Savannah that included some of the African-Americans' accomplishments. During the 70s, he cleaned up this part of the cemetery where the Blacks are buried because the city cleaned only where the Whites were buried. In doing so, he used high school students and anyone else that would volunteer their services. Mr. W.W. law was the President of the NAACP for twenty-six years, and because of his efforts the city now maintains both the north and the south sides of Laurel Grove Cemetery.

Left at End of Median

Mr. W.W. Law was known as the "pissing Postman of Savannah" by his enemies. In the plot you see on the left, he is resting with his grandmother, mother, aunt, and a sister. There is a seashell on his headstone. That is an old African custom: When we leave one world and enter into another we are to take something from the old world with us. The shell is still there, so we can assume that Mr. W.W. Law has not entered into the new world yet.

The Laws' burial plot

Right before Stranger Burial

Can you see the wooden cross directly in front of us? We know that here lie African-Americans, but we do not know their names.

The Stranger Burials marker

On the right are the Slave Burials, we know they were slaves because some of the bodies still had on the shackles. They were not buried here, but in the old Negro burial ground, then exhumed in 1855 and reburied here.

Slaves Burials Marker

On the left, there is the grave of a Mr. Harris; he was a musician, and you see the Confederate Cross in front of his headstone. He was black, and he served in the Confederate Army. The cross was put there by the Daughters of the Confederacy. He could have volunteered, but the records show that he was conscripted into the Confederate army. At the time, many slaves were taken into the Confederate army as servants to their owners. The Confederacy used these instances as propaganda, claiming that the slaves did not want freedom and that they were fighting for the confederacy to preserve slavery. I'm sure you need not be told that these were mostly lies.

The Confederate Cross in front of an African-American grave

Right at Dead End

On the right is the foundation, or bedrock, of the African-American Baptist Church in Georgia.

The bedrock of the African-American church in Georgia

The first grave is that of Rev. Andrew Cox Marshall, the pastor of First African Baptist Church when the present building was started in 1855. Rev. Marshall died in 1856 after completing a fund-raising tour of the North and before the building was finished in 1859.

Rev. Andrew Cox Marshall's grave

The second grave is that of the Rev. Henry C. Cunningham. He was the pastor of Second African Baptist Church on Green Square.

Rev. Henry C. Cunningham's grave

The last grave, with no inscription, is that of Rev. Andrew Bryan. He bought the property where First Bryan Church is

The Rev. Andrew Bryan's grave

located, and his congregationwas started at Brampton Plantation by Rev. George Leile in 1788. First African Baptist, Second African Baptist, and First Bryan Baptist Churches are all from the same congregation started at Brampton Plantation by Rev. George Leile

Right at the Next Street. Exit Cemetery

I told you that Mr. W.W. Law (he always insisted that one use his full name) was known as the "pissing postman of Savannah" by his enemies. He got that name because he refused to use any segregated facilities. Mr. W.W. Law would need to urinate while delivering the mail on occasion, and one day as he relived himself behind a tree, someone saw him and reported his actions. Mr. W.W. Law lost his job, and Robert Kennedy, the Attorney General, helped him get it back. After Mr. W.W. Law got his job back, his admirers made a poster of him with a big smile on his face, his right hand held high. The caption at the bottom of the poster read: "Every shut eye is not sleep, and every good bye is not gone." This was Mr. W.W. Law's way of saying, "You thought you had gotten rid of me, but I'm back." Everyone knew the firing was not about urinating behind a tree, but because of Mr. W.W. Law's civil right's activity. He spent most of his life fighting for equality for African-Americans, and his followers and admirers called him "Mr. Civil Rights."

In 1995, Savannah elected its first African-American mayor, Floyd Adams Jr., and he served two terms. Now, we have another African-American Mayor, Dr. Otis Johnson. Otis Johnson is remembered for integrating Armstrong College. When I was taking a course in African-American history, Dr. Johnson visited our class and said, "While attending Savannah State College, several of my classmates and I decided to integrate Armstrong. We all went over to Armstrong and filled out the papers to enroll. However, on the first day of class I was the only one who showed up, and on graduation day I was the only African-American standing in front of the old Armstrong Building on Bull Street near Gaston across from Forsyth Park."

On 37th St. Crossing Ogeechee Road

The vacant lot on 37th Street where Bobby Hill's house once sat

We are in the Cuyler-Brownville area, where some of the more influential African-Americans lived, including Floyd Adams Sr., the owner of the Savannah Herald and Louis Burke Toomer, who started up Carver State Bank. Over by that blue house is where Bobby Lee Hill lived. He was a lawyer and a civil rights worker. He was the first African-American from Savannah to be elected to the Georgia House of Representatives since reconstruction. During reconstruction, Savannah had two representatives: James Porter and James Merilus Simms. In 1868, these two men were forced out of the Georgia House of Representatives, and in 1870 the Union Army had to come back into Georgia to give these men their seats back. Andrew Young is the man with the distinction of being the first African-American from any part of Georgia to re-enter the Georgia House since reconstruction.

Left onto Harden Street

The Franciscan Handmaids Catholic school

In 1917, the Franciscan Handmaids of the Most Pure Heart of Mary opened the first Catholic school for African-Americans on the West side of Savannah. The Red Brick building on the left housed the school. The building is now being used as a community center. The building on other side is St Mary's, their church, and now it is used only on special occasions.

Right onto 36th Street

On the left is Heritage Place Apartments. Charity Hospital used to be in this building. In 1893 Dr. Alice McKane founded a school for the training of African-American nurses. After her first class graduated, Mrs. McKane and her family left America

The old Charity Hospital site

and went to Liberia in West Africa. After their return to America, Doctors Alice and Cornelius founded McKane Hospital in 1896, which later became Charity Hospital, the first hospital in Savannah built and staffed by African-Americans. Incidentally, Dr. Cornelius McKane was the grandson of King Mannah Funaral of Sierra Leone. This was the same King who sold the land to The American Colonization Society that was used to start the State of Liberia in West Africa.

The yellow house on the right, 611, was once the home of Rev. Ralph Mark Gilbert. This is the house where Martin Luther King Jr. stayed when he was in Savannah during the civil rights movement.

Former residence of Ralph Mark Gilbert

Right onto Burroughs Street

You are now at the corner of 36th Street and Burroughs. When Daddy Grace came to Savannah, he had a lot on 33rd Street and Burroughs. There are houses there now, but he would put up a tent there to preach and heal people. When I was a boy this was routine. Many preachers would preach and heal people. Now I have no idea if these people were being healed, but I do remember people coming to church using a crutch or cane and after being prayed over they had no need of them. Once when Daddy Grace was in Savannah, he began healing people and a Seventh Day Adventist Minister called Daddy Grace a fake and a phony. Daddy Grace told the minister to take it back or he would lock his jaw. The minister took what Daddy Grace said as a threat and called the police. Daddy Grace was arrested, but his followers bailed him out. Daddy grace came back to his tent and preached way into night as if nothing had happened.

Left onto 37th Street

Daddy Grace was a popular person. I remember my aunt telling me of people marching on 37th Street, MLK (which used to be West Broad) and on Victory Drive, and that these processions would be two or three blocks long. The women wore white uniforms, the men would be dressed in dark suits. People would be lined up on both sides of the streets. Daddy Grace had people carrying washtubs near the spectators into which people would toss money.

Johnny Porzio's restaurant was located on the southwest corner of 37th and Montgomery Streets. Porzio refused to serve African-Americans. The only difference between him and Lester Maddox was the he did not use axe handles to chase off the African-American customers; he just closed the restaurant's doors. The restaurant formed an el shape around the building; the red bricks were the outer foundation of the old restaurant. Now, the building is under renovation. Porzio had a small package shop at the end of the building on Montgomery Street, and African-

Former site of Johnny Porzio's restaurant

Americans continued to come and be served through the window for many years, even though they were not allowed entry into his restaurant.

As I was saying, Daddy Grace collected a lot of money. I have no idea of what he did with his money, but he fed many people that were not able to feed themselves, and some of his churches even today still have kitchens or restaurants to feed people.

At the traffic light is Bull Street, which bisects the city, separating east from west.

The white building on the left second from the corner is the Bull Street Library. When Clarence Thomas was going to school in Savannah, he was not allowed to use that library, nor was any other African-Americans at the time.

Bull Street Library

Right onto Abercorn Street

Now, we are in the Thomas Square Neighborhood. One Street over is Lincoln Street, where I have lived here the last thirty years. My last two children grew up in this neighborhood.

Left onto Victory Drive

Victory Drive

Victory Drive is one of the most beautiful Streets in Savannah. The trees hanging over the roadway are live oaks. This wood is very tough, and ship builders used the wood to build ships when wooden ships were in use. The trees grow about eighty feet tall; their branches spread out about one hundred feet; acorns grow on the trees, and squirrels, wild boar, deer, and some birds eat the acorns. That grey stuff that you see hanging from the trees is Spanish moss. It is a parasite, and a member of the pineapple family, and please do not be tempted to take any home with you because there is a small insect that lives in the moss. It is called a chigger. It is very small and hard to see, but if it gets on you, you will know it. It will itch and itch until the little fellow gets its fill of blood, and then it will drop off.

Victory Drive is famous for it palm trees. The azaleas in

bloom in the spring of the year are one of Savannah's most beautiful sites.

Azeleas on Victory Drive

Continuing on Victory Drive at Waters Ave.

As you cross Waters Avenue, if you look to the right and could see ten miles, you would discover the entrance to "The Landings," one of Savannah's first gated communities.

Entrance to the Landings

Continuing on Victory Drive, you will see, on the right, Daffin Park, one of Savannah's largest parks. It comprises about seventy acres. I walk here from my house, then I jog once around this complex, and then walk back home three times a week. Daffin Park itself just finished celebrating its 100th birthday in 2007.

Daffin Park entrance

Also in this complex is Grayson Stadium, home of the Savannah Sand Gnats baseball team. Grayson Stadium is the second oldest minor league stadium in all of baseball. Renovation of the stadium has just been completed, with added seating for the soccer/football field and new public rest rooms.

Grayson Stadium entrance

A Guide to Our Two Savannahs

Daffin Park's Pavilion and Fishpond

Daffin Park's pavilion and fishpond are surrounded by a walking path that is one of Savannah's most beautiful sites. On days when I don't feel up to walking I find a bench and take a seat to enjoy the scenery.

Crossing Skidaway Road

On the right and down Skidaway Road is the only Plantation still in existence in the Savannah area. Wormsloe Planta

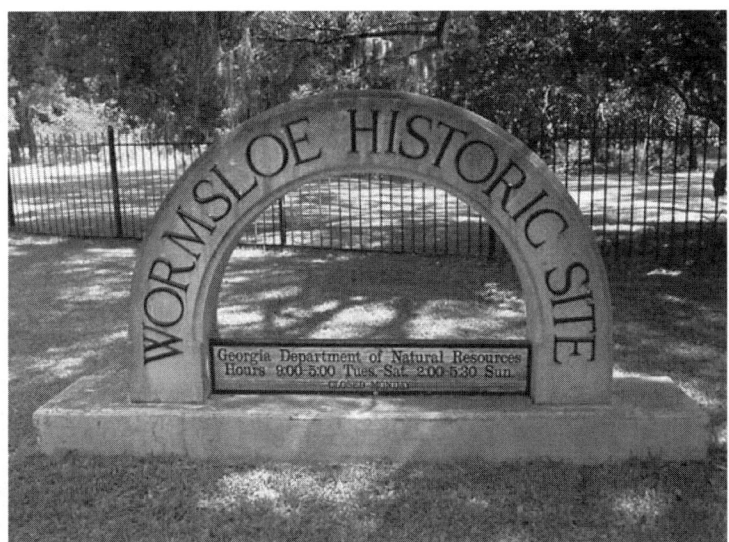

Wormsloe Plantation entrance

tion is a historical site run by the State of Georgia. Part is owned privately by a family, and the family will only allow its part of the plantation to be seen, once a year, around Labor Day. They re-enact the way things were before the civil war. The historical site has a replica of a slave shack and the public is allowed to enter on to part of the old plantation for a fee.

Several miles down that same road, and before you reach Wormsloe platation, you will find Sandfly, a small community where Supreme Court Justice Clarence Thomas grew up. His family still lives in that area, but Mr. Thomas does not come to Savannah often because he is not really popular here.

Sandfly historical marker

A Guide to Our Two Savannahs

Savannah State University Falligate Street entrance

Savannah State University is the first and only African-American college built in Savannah. Savannah State University was first named Georgia State Industrial College for Colored Youth. This college was not started because Georgia wanted a college for African-Americans. In 1887, Georgia State officials found out that white students were attending Atlanta University along with black students, which was a violation of the Glen Bill. The Glen Bill passed the House but not the Senate, so the Glen Bill was not a law, but Georgia tried to enforce it anyway. The Glen Bill was introduced to prevent school integration, and the penalty was one year on the chain gang and a one thousand dollar fine to anyone who allowed integrated classrooms.

In 1890, The Georgia Legislature diverted Atlanta University funds to the opening of Georgia State Industrial College for Colored Youth in Athens, Georgia. Within months, the college was moved to Savannah, and renamed Savannah State Industrial College for Colored Youth.

The oldest building on Savannah State University's campus is Hill Hall. It was constructed in 1901 by the students and faculty under the supervision of Richard R. Wright Sr., the president of the school at the time. It was named after Walter Bernard Hill, the president of the University of Georgia. President William Howard Taft visited Hill Hall in 1912. During World War 1, African-American recruits were trained at this college.

Hill Hall

Savannah State's athletic colors are burnt orange and reflex blue, and their they call themselves the "Tigers." During the 2004-2005 season, the Savannah State men's basketball team earned the dubious honor of being the only second division 1 school since 1955 to play through the entire regular season without winning a single game; the school was referred to as the "winless watch" by ESPN News. Savannah State has more difficulty with its athletic department than most universities do. Their football team did not win one game during the 2006 season either.

Savannah State University sign on campus

A Guide to Our Two Savannahs

In 1976, Donnie Cochran earned a Civil Engineering Degree from Savannah State College (Savannah State University now). In 1985, Lieutenant Cochran became the first African-American to become a member of the Blue Angels Precision Flying Team. Later, in 1994, Lieutenant Commander Cochran assumed command of the Blue Angels, and the Blue Angels Flying Team did not lose one plane under his leadership. This Blue Angel Plane on Savannah State University Campus is in honor of Lieutenant Commander Donnie Cochran.

Blue Angel plane

U-Turn at Plane, Right on Victory Drive

William's Seafood Restaurant was once one of Savannah's favorite eating places. The restaurant burned down a few years ago, and it has not been rebuilt.

Ellis Garvin

Gambling on the river or Dolphin sighting?

    Take your pick: On the left, gambling on the river, or dolphin sightings on the right. Both sports are done on the river. Gambling is done at night, and dolphin sighting is done during the day.

    The beautiful pink building on the right is the Bull River Yacht Club House. A lot of old and new money of Savannah can be found there.

The Bull River Yacht Club clubhouse

Many think that marshes are vast wastelands. Nothing could be farther from the truth. The marshes are a marriage between land and sea; twice a day the sea floods the marshes; twice a day the tides mix salt water with fresh water, and this mixing action stirs up nutrients and recharges the marshes with oxygen.

Left and below: Highway 80 and the marshes

The marshes are ranked as one of nature's most productive ecosystems; they create more organic material per acre than the richest farmland; they provide nurseries and shelters for valuable fish and shellfish, and provide flood protection for the surrounding communities, and finally the marshes supply us with breathing space in our congested coastal areas.

The food source starts with the marsh grasses; the dead grasses break down and mix with algae and other materials creating a kind of rich soup that the marsh animals— shrimp, clams, oysters, and crabs —eat. Then we have the pecking order of the marshes, grasshoppers eat the marsh grasses, spiders, fish, and birds eat the grasshoppers, and after the raccoons and sea birds take their share of the marsh bounty. We fish the seas and dig the oyster and clam beds hoping to claim our share of nature's bounty.

We humans depend on the marshes far more than you would expect because two-thirds of all commercial fish and shellfish need the protection of the coastal marshes to survive. In fact, the experts believe that one of the reasons our seas are being depleted of fish is because of the destruction of coastal wetlands.

Left onto Campbell Avenue

Now, two hundred years before General Oglethorpe came to the colony of Georgia in 1733, the Spaniards had claimed the area from Port Royal, South Carolina, to St. Augustine, Florida, as Spanish Territory, naming it La Florida or Bimini, looking to establish the first colony in the new world.

Left onto Van Horn Drive

When General Oglethorpe began the colony of Georgia, he established the first permanent structure on Tybee Island, a ninety-foot tall lighthouse designed by Noble Jones of Wormsloe Plantation, as you see here, and a stronghold named Fort Tybee was established near the lighthouse. During this period, the island was used as a hiding place for pirates such as Blackbeard. Today beachcombers patiently scan the beaches with metal detectors looking for buried treasure.

Right onto Meddin Drive

During the American Revolutionary War, the French Fleet, the greatest gathering of foreign ships ever assembled in American waters, anchored off Tybee Island in support of American Patriots in their losing effort to take Savannah back from the British.

Also during the antebellum plantation era, the lighthouse site was a popular place for duels between South Carolina's "Southern gentlemen" who used pistols to settle their differences.

In 1819, President James Monroe traveled from Savannah to Tybee on the "SS Savannah", which later became the first steamship to cross the Atlantic Ocean.

Fort Screven

Tybee Lighthouse

In the fall of 1861, the Confederate Forces abandoned Fort Screven, set fire to the stairs of the Tybee Island Lighthouse, and pulled back to Fort Pulaski. This gave the Union Forces an opportunity to set up eleven Artillery Batteries to later attack Fort Pulaski.

The Tybee Lighthouse was one of the first public structures built in Georgia. It was completed in 1736, and its 90-foot height made it the loftiest in America. Storms destroyed the first and second lighthouses built on Tybee Island. In 1773, the third lighthouse was built, and this is that lighthouse. In 1861, The Confederate forces abandoned Fort Screven and burned the wooden stairs up in this lighthouse before retreating to Fort Pulaski hoping to make it useless to the Union Forces.

U Turn onto Meddin Drive

When slaves first entered the Colony of Georgia from Africa or other foreign ports their first stop would be at the Lazaretto. or quarantine center. It is said to have been located three miles away from the Tybee light house, but the exact site is unknown.

Lazaretto

Left onto Van Horn Drive

After the slaves had been checked for diseases and fatted up, then they would be taken in shackles and chains to the baracoons on River Street and on into the squares of Savannah to be sold.

Old Tybee Island House

If you will notice, this old Tybee Island house is built up off the ground. This not done for looks; when storms visit Tybee Island on occasion, the island is flooded.

Right onto Campbell Avenue

New Tybee Island House

This is a newer house built off the ground to meet the new building code on Tybee Island. Some people close in the stilts that support the house and use the space as a garage. I told you about how real estate prices have gone up in downtown Savannah, but here prices have done even better.

Right onto US 80

Cockspur Island light house

To the right is Cockspur Island Lighthouse. Florence Martus, the Waving Girl, did her waving on nearby Elba Island, not on River Street. Her brother was the lighthouse keeper on Cockspur Island.

Fort Pulaski

Fort Pulaski was completed in 1847. It was named after Casimir Pulaski the highest-ranking foreign officer to die fighting on the side of the colonists during the siege of Savannah in 1779. The fort is located on Cockspur Island. Robert E. Lee's first assignment after graduating from West Point was to drain the marsh and select a site for Fort Pulaski. The fort was built on a marsh. Timbers had to be driven sixty to seventy feet down in the mud for the foundation. They used twenty-five million bricks, and many were Savannah-gray bricks. The slaves made these bricks and shipped them down the Savannah River from Hermitage Plantation on barges. Even today there is a noticeable difference in the Savannah gray bricks and the other bricks used in the construction of Fort Pulaski. They used over twenty-five hundred slaves to help build Fort Pulaski, leased from the surrounding plantation owners.

A moat completely surrounds Fort Pulaski. Drawbridge on the right for entry

In 1861, Georgia's Governor Brown ordered the occupation of Fort Pulaski. At the time, there were only two men manning the fort. General Lee thought that Fort Pulaski's seven and half-foot walls were unbreachable by cannon fired from Tybee Island, which was over a mile away. He told Colonel Charles Olmstead, the commander of the fort: "They may make it warm for you, but they can not breach the walls of the fort." At the time, regular bore canons were not accurate, and over a mile away were beyond their effective reach.

The fort's northeast wall that was breached

A Guide to Our Two Savannahs

In the fall of 1861, Union forces took possession of Tybee Island and began to put gun batteries in place to start an assault on Fort Pulaski across Lazaretto Creek. After thirty hours of shelling from the new rifled-barrel canons of the Union troops, the fort's northeast wall was breached. Colonel Charles Olmstead thought that a shell from the Union troops would hit the powder magazine in the southwest wall of the fort and kill everyone in the fort. To avoid this fate, he surrendered Fort Pulaski to the Union forces.

In 1862, General David Hunter issued general order #7, freeing all the slaves at the fort, in all of Georgia, South Carolina, and Florida. Almost immediately, President Lincoln rescinded General Hunter's order, but this brave order on the General's part may have helped President Lincoln issue his Emancipation Proclamation a year later. Three things happened for the first time here at Tybee and Fort Pulaski. This was the first time rifled-canons were used by the Union Forces; the slaves at Fort Pulaski were the first to be freed in Georgia' and for the first time the ex-slaves at the fort would be paid for their labor.

When General Quincy Gilmore took command of Fort Pulaski, he used Marsh Hanes, a former slave and riverboat pilot, to keep him informed of the activity in the Savannah harbor. Mr. Hanes also directed slaves to Fort Pulaski, and Fort Pulaski became a stop on the Underground Railroad which helped many slaves to move north. In 1863, , General David Hunter organized the First Volunteers of South Carolina, the "Freedom Fighters." These were the first African-Americans from the South to officially fight in the Union Army.

Before the Union troops took Fort Pulaski, there were two African-Americans who furnished Fort Pulaski with seafood and fresh meat. Anthony Odingsells was a fisherman, and he took care of the fort's seafood needs. Davis was a butcher, and he took care of the fort's fresh meat needs. Both of these men owned slaves of their own. Odingsells owned about ten, and Davis owned about six. The slaves owned by these two African-Americans were used to make money for their owners, the same way the plantation owners used them.

Now, there were other African-Americans who owned slaves, but the slaves they owned were mostly family members. For example, a slave would buy his own freedom, and then he would buy his wife's freedom, next the freedom of his children. Now you may want to know, why not buy the family members and free them? There were many penalties for being a free African-American. A free African-American had to pay a ten dollar registration fee, fifty cents per year to work, pay more taxes than non African-Americans, donate two or three days a month to public works projects, have a white guardian, carry papers stating that he was free, and live in fear of being sold back into slavery by any white that wanted to make a quick buck.

Bonaventure Cemetery's entrance

On the right, sitting on a high bluff is Bonaventure Cemetery, and buried there is the great composer and native son of Savannah, Mr. Johnny Mercer. He wrote the lyrics to more than 1000 songs, such as: "In the Cool, Cool, Cool of the Evening," "On the Acheson, Topeka and the Santa Fe," "Moon River," "Days of Wine and Roses" and many others. Also, this was once the home of the "Bird Girl." Now, she resides at the Telfair Museum, and the reason for her departure from Bonaventure Cemetery is because of the popularity of the book and movie

Midnight in the Garden of Good and Evil. The "Bird Girl" was pictured on the cover of the book, and that popularity made many visitors to Savannah want to see her. So for her own protection, she was moved to the Telfair Museum.

There were three classifications of African-Americans in Savannah. First, the slave who lived on the plantation; second, the slave who hired himself out and lived in the alleys or any place he could find to live and had to give a percentage of his earning to his owner; third, the free African-American who lived on his own. The African-American with the most freedom was the African-American who hired himself out, because his owner might not see him for six months or even a year.

Right onto Abercorn Street

Now, I am aware of only one African-American who sold slaves in Savannah. Abraham Beasley was his name, and he was married to Matilda Beasley. Several people have said to me, "Mother Beasley would not be married to any slaver." The problem with their rebuttal is Mother Beasley could not be married to anyone and be a nun. She became a nun after her husband Abraham Beasley died.

Coming up on the right is the oldest hospital built for African-Americans in all of North America, the Georgia Infirmary. It was built in 1832. A non African-American, Thomas Williams, gave fourteen acres of land and the money to the city to build the Georgia Infirmary with the understanding that the property is used for the betterment of African-Americans. Should the property be used for any other purpose the property will revert back to his heirs.

So, you will always see the name Georgia Infirmary, although, St. Joseph's/Chandler Hospital operates the facility now. In the beginning, the hospital used African-American nurses but no African-American doctors. The infirmary is now being used to help find ways to help African-Americans control hypertension.

Mr. Williams was a businessman and a minister. His being

The Georgia Infirmary historical marker

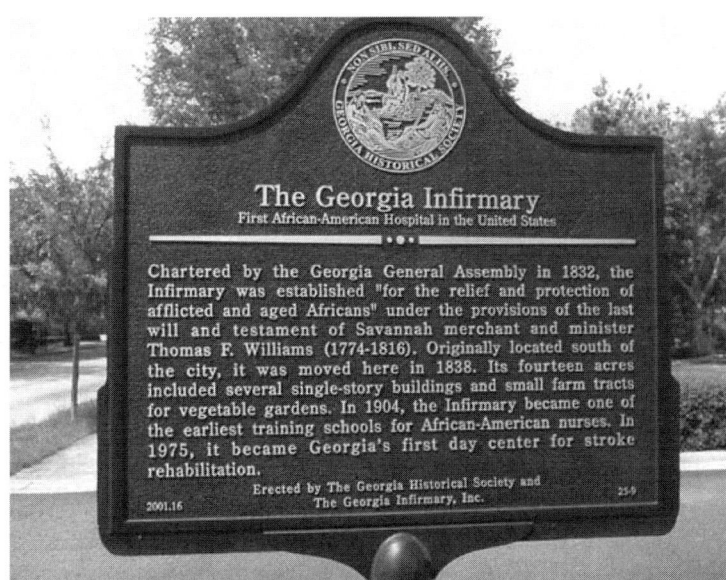

Site of the old Georgia Infirmary

a Christian may have helped him recognize the plight of the slaves. Slaves were fed worse than convicts or prisoners. The slaves worked long hours, twelve to sixteen hours a day; their clothing and housing were inadequate. Many slaves were in bad health by the time they reached the age of forty-five or fifty, and on the plantations a food allowance was given only to the slaves able to work.

On two occasions, the Georgia legislature tried to pass a law that would have the State of Georgia take care of the slaves that were unable to work, but it failed passage because the State wanted the slave owners to share the cost. The Georgia Infirmary is the result of that effort, and the state paid the Georgia Infirmary twenty dollars per patient per year.

Right onto Anderson Street

Former office of Robbie Robertson

The second building from the corner on the right, the tan building with maroon shutters, was once the office of Robbie

Robertson, an attorney for the NAACP. As we make the turn, it will be on your left. In 1989, Mr. Robertson was sitting at his desk opening his mail when a letter blew up, knocking out all the windows on the first floor of the building and at the same time killing Mr. Robertson. Later, law enforcement found that the letter was sent by a racist from Alabama. They also found that the racist had sent another letter to a judge in Alabama. The Alabama judge died the same way that Mr. Robertson did—by opening his mail. The racist had sent mail bombs to others, but the other people were more fortunate and did not lose their lives as the judge and Mr. Robertson did. Now, just remember that this happened fewer than twenty years ago. There is still much racial hatred alive and well in America.

SCAD Building

SCAD Diner

A Guide to Our Two Savannahs

Bobbies is one of SCAD's Diners; Bobbies is on the East side and they have another one on the West side. The above images show two examples of SCAD's efforts to renovate old and abandoned structures in the downtown area of Savannah.

Old St. Pius X High School

Coming up at the light is East Broad, the eastern boundary of colonial Savannah. At that time the area of the city totalled two point two square miles. Savannah now comprises sixty and a half square miles, all in Chatham County.

Straight ahead over that rise and on the right is the building that was St. Pius X High School, the school that Clarence Thomas, Associate Justice of the Supreme Court, and Floyd Adams Jr., the first African-American mayor of Savannah attended.

Left onto East Broad Street

On the right, the yellow building was once one of the better African-American grocery stores in old Savannah. It was owned by a Mr. Duncan Pringle, and the white building with the diamonds at the top was once Gusman's Record Shop. If you wanted an old record, Gusman would find it for you, but the new malls and the changing times have put Mr. Gusman out of business.

Mr. Pringle's old grocery store

Left onto Henry Street

The Carnegie Library is on your left. If you look above the door you will see representations of the seven men who started this first library for African-Americans in Savannah. It was started in another building and at another location. Later, they got a grant from the Carnegie Institution and built this library, hence

The Carnegie Library

the name. A few years ago this library was in desperate need of repairs, and we African-Americans had much difficulty raising money for this worthwhile venture. However, we can and do spend over a billion dollars a year on hair dye.

Right onto Habersham Street

The board members were reviewing their options when, out of the blue, an anonymous donor offered over a millions dollar to help with the renovation if they would add a wing onto the library and call it the Clarence Thomas wing. This offer made the board members begin to fight amongst themselves; the president of the board threatened to quit the board because he thought that Clarence Thomas' name should not be put on anything; he wrote the newspaper a long letter explaining his position. He was against accepting the money.

Right onto Gwinnet Street

I even wrote the paper; I agreed with the president of the board, and I said, "I would rather drink muddy water and sleep in a hollow log than put Clarence Thomas' name on anything."

I did not make that up; I got it from one of the old blues songs. Most African-Americans think that Clarence Thomas is an intelligent person, and he is just as qualified as anyone else to be an associate justice on the Supreme Court, but we are unable to understand how he could be against affirmative action when affirmative action is the reason he is an associate justice on the Supreme Court today.

I know you are interested in what happened with the money. The money won as always, because Carnegie Library has a new and modern wing called the "Clarence Thomas Wing," with all the amenities of any modern library.

Left onto East Broad Street

The building across the street on our right as we make the turn was once the Melody Theater. It was the first air-conditioned theater built (1946) for African-Americans in Savannah.

This became the place where the jazz bands came to perform.

Melody Theater

Remember the two Savannahs? On the right is Prince Hall and this is where the African-Americans Masonic members go to attend their meetings.

Prince Hall

Left onto East Huntington Street

Now, we are in the Beach Institute neighborhood, and the houses that you see here have been renovated and renamed Robbie Robertson Housing, after the civil-rights attorney who was blown up by the mail bomb.

King-Tisdale cottage

On the right is the King-Tisdell Cottage. It is an African-American museum. Its function is to preserve the African-American culture of the 1890s. See the hitching post. This is not a new house. This house was not built on its present site but on Ott Street. Inside, you will find documents such as advertisements for slaves and the bill of sale for slaves, and many of the things that were used in the 1890s.

Right onto Habersham Street

In the backyard there is a fountain called "Free to Fly." The drain was made from shackles once used to hold slaves. There is a fish on the side of the fountain that appears to be swimming upstream as the water spills over the side of the fountain, and there is a bird on the top of the fountain.

I have always believed that this fountain was inspired by the belief that the old African-Americans were able to fly. Toni Morrison wrote a book call "Song of Solomon" on this same theme.

The frame houses in this area are built in the Victorian Style, and Colonel John DeVeaux from the Custom House lived in this neighborhood, and also Jane DeVeaux who was not his wife but probably a relative of his family. She ran an underground school.

First Congregational Church

This is Whitefield Square, and the white building on your left is First Congregational Church. It was built by the American Missionary Association. The members of this church were the teachers of Beach Institute, their students, and their student's parents. Beach Institute had Black and White teachers.

On the left are Rose of Sharon Apartments, where the Old Negro burial grounds once were located. It is from this site that the "stranger burials" and the "slave burials" were exhumed and reburied at Laurel Grove Cemetery in 1855.

Rose of Sharon Apartments

Next is Troup Square, and the French Gothic church on the left is the Unitarian Universal Church, once St Stephen's Church, the church attended by the lighter-skinned African-Americans. This building was not built here but moved from Oglethorpe Square. It is also known as the "Jingle Bell Church" because its musical director, Mr. Pierpont, wrote the song "Jingle Bells."

Unitarian Universal Church— "Jingle Bells Church"

Right onto Liberty Street

We are still in the Beach Institute neighborhood. It gets its name from Beach Institute which was built in 1867.

Right onto Price Street

It was built by the Freedman's Bureau, American Missionary Association. Mr. Alfred E. Beach gave the money to buy the land. He was the inventor of the first typewriter for the blind and the first subway system in New York City.

Left onto Harris Street Lane

Beach Institute

The building on the right is Beach Institute; the first school on the east side built for African-Americans. Mrs. Susie King Taylor had a private school in this area and Beach Institute put her school out of business. Beach Institute was free, but they did expect the students and their parents to attend First Congregational Church, so that they could convert the students and their parents to their way of thinking. Many African-Americans did not like going to First Congregational Church, but they were unable to pay the fifty cents or a dollar per student per month to attend Mrs. Taylor's school. Remember, right after the Civil War African-Americans were making about two cents per hour, and sometimes not even that because many plantation owners would promise the worker a food allowance, clothing, and twenty-five dollars after the harvest; however, many workers never got the twenty-five dollars.

Left onto East Broad Street

Directly in front of us and across the street, there was a train switching yard, and many people say that there was a passenger terminal here, but I don't remember that; however, I do remember there being a freight yard here. The tracks came in from Albany, Georgia, and they were owned by the Seaboard Coast Line. This was a place of employment for many people of the area.

During slavery, Slaves cleared and laid more than a thousand miles of track in Georgia. Some of that track is still in use today.

Old freight yard

Left onto Liberty Street

Over on the right is the Fred Wessel's Projects, and they are some of the best-looking housing projects that I have seen any

Ellis Garvin

Fred Wessel's projects

where in the country. Notice, they have no broken or boarded-up windows, which is a common sight in most projects.

Next Right onto Houston

Crawford Square is the only square that still has a cistern. You can see the cavity. Once all the squares had these cisterns, and water from them was used by the fire brigade, which was made up of slaves. This is the last square that still has any of the fencing left. All squares at one time had fencing. This is also the only square that ever had a basketball court. Some time ago, the new people in the neighborhood complained about the noise of the basketball players. They wanted the basketball hoops taken down, but the mayor and city council said, "No!" The basketball court was a part of Savannah's history. The hoops would stay up.

Circle Greene Square

We are entering Greene Square. The green house was the house of Rev. Cunningham when he was the pastor of Second African Baptist Church, on our left.

Former home of Rev. Henry Cox Cunningham

Second African Baptist Church is where General Sherman issued field order # 15, which became better known as the "Forty acres and a mule" promise. Shortly after, Rev. Ulysses L. Houston led one thousand newly freed slaves to Skidaway Island and began to farm the land and set up a town. Later, General Sherman's "Forty acres and a mule" promise was broken, and Rev Houston and his followers had to give up their town and leave Skidaway Island.

Second African Baptist Church

A marker on Greene Square

The marker above, in Greene Square, clearly states: "General William T. Sherman and Secretary of War Edwin M. Stanton met with the Negroes of this city and the newly freed slaves at Second African Baptist Church when Savannah surrendered to General Sherman in December 1864." I make a point of this because there are others who say that this meeting never took place at Second African Baptist Church, but at the Green-Meldrim House, General Sherman's headquarters.

The Rev. Martin Luther King

Martin Luther King Jr. gave his "I have a Dream Speech" at the Second African Baptist Church, before giving it in Washington DC.

Meldrim House, General Sherman's headquarters.

Right on President Street, Going East

We are on President Street, and up at the traffic light is East Broad. In 1863, long before General Sherman reached Savannah, Mr. William Pollard was asked to gather all the slaves in the area at President and East broad Streets, and Mr. James Porter read President Lincoln's Emancipation Proclamation.

Right onto East Broad Street

When we reach the next corner, the steeples of St. John the Baptist Cathedral will be visible on our left above the houses.

Right onto Oglethorpe Avenue

The cathedral of St. John the Baptist is one of the most beautiful churches in Savannah. I recommend visiting this church, time permitting.

Coming up on the left is the main police station in Savannah. In 1947, Rev. Ralph Mark Gilbert got the signatures of 19,000 African-Americans and took them to the officials of City Hall. He got them to hire nine African-American policemen and six city workers. The policemen were not allowed to wear their

The steeples of St. John the Baptist cathedral

Savannah-Chatham metropolitan police department

uniforms back and forth to work; they were not allowed to carry guns, nor were they allowed to arrest non-African-Americans. They were the first African-American policemen hired in the state of Georgia.

Big Ben

On the left. You will find a big bell in front of the firehouse. All the squares of Savannah had a bell like this at one time. It was used to alert the people of danger. such as fire, the British are coming, or the Indians are coming. The people would come to the square to lend their service.

On the right is Juliette Gordon Low's birthplace. Lowe founded the Girl Scouts of America. This house was built for James Moore Wayne in 1820. He was the first Supreme Court Justice from Savannah, Georgia.

Does anyone remember Dred Scott? James Moore Wayne

Juliette Gordon Lowe House

was on the Supreme Court when the Dred Scott case came before it. Dred Scott was a slave who traveled with his owner through free territories such as Illinois and Wisconsin. When his owner died, he tried to buy his own freedom from his owner's widow, but she refused and hired him out. Mr. Scott then sued for his freedom; it took ten years for his case to come before the Supreme Court. In 1847. The Supreme Court was made up of nine justices. Seven of the justices were appointed by southern Presidents, and five of them owned slaves. Chief Justice Roger B. Taney was a staunch supporter of slavery, and he wrote the opinion of Court: Dred Scott, being black, had no right to sue for his freedom because he was colored and would never be able to become a citizen of the United States of America. Sometime later, the son of Dred Scott's owner bought his and his wife's freedom.

That was not the end of the Dred Scott case. In 1860 when Abraham Lincoln was trying to win the primary for the Republican nomination for the Presidency of the United States of America, he campaigned against the Dred Scott decision, and many think that this case had some bearing on the Civil War. Undoubtedly, this case drove a wedge between the North and the South. The North knew that it could not compete with slave labor, and the South wanted to take slavery all the way to the Pacific Ocean.

Now, you may have two questions: How could such a beautiful city have such a dark horrid past, and the other would be, Do we still have two Savannahs?

The first question is easy to answer; greed will make humans do things that logic can never explain, and the second question I would like to answer the way that Mr. W.W. Law might have answered it. From slavery to now, we have made a tremendous amount of progress; however, real, every-day equality is still a commodity that is just beyond the reach of the average African-American.

A restaurant with a door for "white" and a separate door for "colored"

We do not need the signs that read Colored and White anymore as the restaurant above has, or Union Station had when I was a boy. For example, I was in Hawaii several years ago and we checked into the Four Seasons, a five-star hotel. The girls put a real flower lei around each of our necks, gave each of us a damp cold towel to freshen up with, and a big cold glass of the best tasting juice ever. And all before we signed in.

I wanted to know the cost of a room. Not that I was paying, because my daughter's husband worked for the Four Seasons at the time, and our rooms were all gratis.

The lowest price room was four hundred and ninety-five dollars per night, and I do not believe that they had a limit. If you could pay, they would make every effort to provide the service of your choice.

Left onto Fahm Street

Georgia's motto "Non Sebi Sed Aliis" surrounds the seal at the top of this marker

Laurel Grove South Cemetery

In 1853, the city reserved 4 acres in the new Laurel Grove Cemetery for Savannah's African-American community. This new burial ground replaced an older black cemetery located near Whitefield Square. Pastors Andrew Bryan (First Colored Baptist Church) and Henry Cunningham (Second Baptist Church) were among those whose bodies were moved to the new location. Here are buried many of Savannah's prominent black leaders-- educators, civic/community leaders, Masons, politicians, entrepreneurs, and religious leaders. Later increased in acreage by the city, it continues in use today.

Erected by The Georgia Historical Society and the Friends of Laurel Grove South Cemetery

Remember the inscription in the circle on the top of this historical market: "Non sebi sed aliis!" That is Georgia's Motto, and it means, "Not for themselves but others." The slaves could not have written it, because most slaves did not know how to read or write. In fact, Mr. James Simms was beaten in public for teaching slaves to read. So, the slave owners had to be the ones that wrote Georgia's motto. That's strange, because the slaves were the only ones who lived by Georgia's motto. Most of the antebellum mansions were built with slave labor in Savannah and throughout the South, and the owners of these mansions got their wealth and financial stability at the expense of the slaves laboring in the cane fields, cotton fields, and rice paddies. The slaves labored, "Not for themselves but others!" Is that not ironic?

One last tidbit of information. On December 22, 1864,

Major General Sherman gave the city of Savannah, 150 heavy guns with plenty of ammunition, and about 2500 bales of cotton to President Lincoln as a Christmas gift. That cotton would have been stored in the Visitors Center parking lot and in the warehouses that the Savannah College of Art and Design now uses as classrooms.

What did you see and hear on this tour that you should keep for the rest of your life? You don't have to answer, "The slaves of barracoons!" Most of us will remember them as just another horror of our past, but we could remember them as the strength of our past. The slaves that passed through the barracoons never gave up, and the next time you come to an impasse, and hope is gone, and defeat is on the horizon, remember "the slaves of the barracoons." They made it through those horrific times. We are living proof of their will of survival. They did it, and so can we.

Thanks for allowing me to share our two Savannahs with you. We do look forward to your return with your family and friends at a later date. Enjoy the remainder of you stay in Savannah!

Savannah's Beautiful Squares

To truly enjoy Savannah's squares, one must walk into the square and acclimate oneself to the square's past. Then the enjoyment begins.

Elbert and Liberty: the Two Lost Squares

Elbert Square was located on Montgomery Street between West Hull and West Perry Streets. It was laid out in 1801. It was named in honor of Samuel Elbert, planter and revolutionary warrior. The Civic Center now sits on this site. The Flame of Freedom once lived here. Later, the flame was moved to Liberty Square. The Chatham County Court House now occupies the old site of Liberty Square. It was laid out in 1799 and named to celebrate the freedom and independence gained through the Revolution and to honor the "Sons of Liberty" who fought for that independence. The "Flame of Freedom" remains in front of the Chatham County Court House. Elbert and Liberty Squares are the two lost squares.

Franklin Square

Franklin Square is located on Montgomery Street between West Bryan and West Congress Streets. It was laid out in 1791 and was named in honor of Benjamin Franklin. Franklin Square was once referred to as Water Tower or Reservoir Square, because of its water tower. The First African Baptist Church is on the northwest side of the square. The church is the oldest brick African-American Church in North America.

Chatham Square

Chatham Square is located on Barnard Street between West Taylor and West Gordon Streets; it was laid out in 1847. It was named in honor of William Pitt, the Earl of Chatham. The Louis Burke Toomer (treasurer and founder of Carver State Bank) Memorial is in this square. The old Barnard Street School is on the Northwest corner. Today, it is part of the Savannah College of Art and Design building.

Pulaski Square

Pulaski Square is located on Barnard Street between West Harris and West Charlton Street. It was laid out in 1837. It was named in honor of Count Casimir Pulaski, the highest ranking-officer to die in the American Revolution. The old Jewish Education Alliance Building is on this square (now a SCAD dormitory). The Francis Bartow House is also faces this square.

Orleans Square

Orleans Square is located on Barnard Street between West Hull and West Perry Streets. It was laid out in 1815. It was named to honor the American victory at New Orleans in January 1815. The German Memorial Fountain is in this square. The Champion-McAlpin House is on the southeast side of square.

Telfair Square

Telfair Square is located on Barnard Street between West State and West York Streets. It was laid out in 1733. For the first 150 years it was called St. James Square, in one of the most fashionable areas in Savannah. It was renamed to honor the Telfair Family. The Telfair Academy of Arts and Sciences, the Jepson Center for the Arts, and Methodist Trinity Church are on this square, and the Girl Scouts Monument is in the southeast corner of the square.

Ellis Square

Ellis Square is located on Barnard Street between West Bryan and West Congress Streets. It was laid out in 1733. It was named in honor of Henry Ellis, Georgia's second Royal Governor. This square was also known as Market Square because of its use as a wholesale food stuffs market.

Monterey Square

Monterey Square is located on Bull Street between Taylor and Gordon Streets; it was laid out in 1847. It was named in honor of the battle of Monterey, in the Mexican-American war. The Temple Mickve Israel is on this square, as is the Mercer-Wilder House (designed by John Norris). The Mercer Wilder House was the home of Jim Williams, the central character in the movie "Midnight in the Garden of Good and Evil." The Pulaski Monument is in the center of the square.

Madison Square

Madison Square is located on Bull Street between Harris and Charlton Streets. It was laid out in 1837. It was named in honor of President James Madison. St. John's Episcopal Church, the Sergeant Jasper monument, and the Green-Meldrim House are located on this square. The Green-Meldrim House was General Sherman's headquarters. This, and not the Second African Baptist Church, is where some think General Sherman met with Garrison Frazier and nineteen other African-Americans to discuss the needs of the newly-freed slaves.

Chippewa Square

Chippewa Square is located on Bull Street between Hull and Perry Streets; it was laid out in 1815. This square was named in honor of a battle of the War of 1812. The bench from the Forrest Gump movie was on the north side of this square. The James Edward Oglethorpe Monument is in the center of square. Also, First Baptist Church and the Savannah Theater, designed by William Jay and the oldest theater in America, are on this square.

Wright Square

Wright Square is located on Bull Street between State and York Streets. It was laid out in 1733. This square was first named in honor of Viscount Percival, later the Earl of Egmont. It was later renamed to honor James Wright, Georgia's last Royal Governor. It was commonly called Courthouse Square because there has always been a courthouse on this site. The yellow brick courthouse was designed by William Gibbons Preston. The Lutheran Church of the Ascension and the US Federal Building are on this square. The Washington Gordon Monument is in the center of the square along with Tomochichi's grave and a big boulder that once rested on it. Hosea Williams was arrested from atop Tomochichi's boulder during a civil rights gathering.

Johnson Square

Johnson Square is located on Bull Street between Bryan and Congress Streets; it was laid out in 1733. This was the first square completed. It was named in honor of Robert Johnson, Royal Governor of South Carolina when Georgia was founded. Christ Church—Anglican, now Episcopal—was built in 1750, the first house of worship in Georgia. Savannah's first skyscraper, two East Bryan Street, and the Nathaniel Greene Monument can be found on this square.

Calhoun Square

Calhoun Square is located on Abercorn Street between East Taylor and East Gordon streets. It was laid out in 1815. It was named in honor of John C. Calhoun, a South Carolina politician and Secretary of War. Wesley Monumental Church and Massie School are on this square. Incidentally, the Massie School is the oldest remaining building of Georgia's public school system.

Lafayette Square

Lafayette Square is located on Abercorn Street between East Harris and East Charlton Streets; it was laid out in 1837. It was named in honor of the Marquis de Lafayette. The Andrew Low House, Flannery O'Connor's childhood home (marker in front), and St. John the Baptist Cathedral are on this square. The Battersby-Hartridge House is the only significant Charleston style house in the city. Also, the Hamilton Turner House (now an Inn) was the first residence to have electricity in the city. This house was featured in the book "Midnight in the Garden of Good and Evil." The Andrew Low House is on this square, along with its carriage house, where the girl scouts began.

Oglethorpe Square

Oglethorpe Square is located on Abercorn Street between East State and East York Streets; it was laid out in 1742. It was named in honor of James Edward Oglethorpe, the founder of the Georgia colony. The Owen-Thomas House is on this square. This house is believed to be the finest example of regency architecture in the United States. Designed by William Jay, it was the first house in Savannah to have indoor plumbing. This mansion still has its slave quarters intact.

Reynolds Square

Reynolds Square is located on Abercorn Street between East Bryan and East Congress Streets. It was named in honor of John Reynolds, Georgia's first Royal Governor. The Filature House, or silk house, was later used as a meeting place because there was no silk to process. The Pink House, one of the few houses that did not get burned during the fire of 1796, and the Oliver Sturgess House are on this square. Sturgess was a partner in the Steam Ship Savannah venture. Also, the Lucas Theater can be found here.

Whitfield Square

Whitfield Square is located on Habersham Street between East Taylor and East Gordon streets. It was laid out in 1851. It was named in honor of the Rev. George Whitfield, founder of Bethesda orphanage. The First Congregational Church, the Rose of Sharon apartments, and the site of the old Negro Burial Ground, and the Red Cross Building are found on this square.

Troup Square

Troup Square is located on Habersham Street between East Harris and East Charlton Streets. It was laid out in 1851. It was named in honor of George Michael Troup, US Representative, Governor, and US Senator. The naming of Troup Square was done while Mr. Troup was still alive. The high stoop McDonough row houses are on the east side of this square. The Unitarian Universal Church is on the West side of the square, and the Armillary Sphere is in the center of the square.

Columbia Square

Columbia Square is located on Habersham Street between East State and East York streets. It was laid out in 1799. This square takes the poetic name of our country. The Davenport House (an excellent example of Federalist styling), the Abraham Sheftall house (now the Historic Savannah Foundation), and the Wormsloe Fountain (in the center of square) are found on this square.

Warren Square

Warren Square is located on Habersham Street between East Bryan and East Congress Streets. It was laid out in 1791. This square is named in honor of General Joseph Warren, killed in the 1775 Battle at Bunker Hill. On St. Julian Street, between this square and Washington Square, are some of the oldest houses in the historic district.

Crawford Square

Crawford Square is located on Houston Street between East Hull and East Perry Streets. It was laid out in 1841. This square was named in honor of William Harris Crawford, Secretary of the Treasury under President Madison. This square is the only one to have a basketball court and it still has its Cistern in place. At one time, all squares had cisterns to hold water to fight fires.

Greene Square

Greene Square is located on Houston Street between East State and East York streets; it was named in honor of General Nathaniel Greene, second in command to General George Washington during the Revolutionary War. The Second African Baptist Church, where General Sherman issued Field Order 15, and Rev. Martin Luther King, Jr. made his "I Have a Dream" speech before making it in Washington DC, is on this square.

Washington Square

Washington Square is located on Houston Street between East Bryan and East Congress Streets. This square was named in honor of George Washington, first President of the United States. This honor was bestowed upon him while he was still alive. This square was once the site of the biggest New Year's Eve bonfires; many fires were higher than the buildings around the square. The Seaman's House and the Mulberry Inn, which was once a cotton warehouse, are on this square. St. Julian Street, on the left side of the square, is paved with "tabby" (a mixture of oyster shells, sand, lime, and water).

Savannah's Must See Places

Courthouse on Wright Square
(Bull and East York Streets)

This courthouse was designed by William Gibbons Preston. The citizens of Savannah will visit this courthouse once or twice during their lives, because this is where birth, marriage, and death certificates are issued. Too bad this yellow brick court house cannot talk, because if it could it would tell of all the African-American families broken apart by being sold to different buyers. The slavers would build a platform in front of this courthouse to display the slaves to be sold. Slave owners would whip their slaves on the same platform; the public whipping was intended to intimidate the other slaves. This square was also known as Courthouse Square.

Owen-Thomas House
(Abercorn and East President Streets)

    The Owen-Thomas House was designed by William Jay in 1819. This house was the first in Savannah to have indoor plumbing, and this house is still thought to be the best example of Regency architecture in all of North American. There are daily tours.

Old Stables and Slave Quarters
(Abercorn and East President Streets)

The Owen-Thomas Carriage House is where the horses were stabled, and the slave quarters are above the stables. This is Savannah's best example of the contrast of living conditions between slaves and their owners: The Owen-Thomas House and the Slave Quarters are operated as a museum, and there are daily tours.

Beach Institute
(Price and East Harris Streets)

The Beach Institute was built in 1867. Mr. Alfred E. Beach gave the money to purchase the land, and it was built by the Freedman's Bureau and the American Missionary Association. Now, Beach Institute is a museum and it has a prize collection of wood carvings done by Mr. Ulysses Davis. They conduct daily tours.

Davenport House
(East State and Habersham Streets)

The Davenport House is an excellent example of a Federalist style house. It was designed and built by Mr. Davenport. He had nine slaves who lived in the house with his family. It's a museum and there are daily tours.

First African Baptist Church
(Montgomery and West Bryan Streets)

The First African Baptist Church was built in 1859. It was a stop on the Underground Railroad and a great example of African-American commitment. There are daily tours.

St. John the Baptist Cathedral
(Abercorn and East Harris Streets)

St. John the Baptist Cathedral is one of the most beautiful churches in Savannah. Inside it has fourteen Stations of the Cross, and all hand carved in wood. The public is allowed entry if the church is not having services.

Jepson Center
(Barnard and West York Streets)

The Jepson Center is Savannah's newest art gallelry. On my first and only visit here, I saw a painting done in sand by the Tibetan Monks. The Jepson Center always has something new and surprising to offer. The museum has daily tours.

Ships of the Sea Maritime Museum
(Martin Luther King Blvd. between St. Julian and Broughton Streets)

If you have an interest in ships, this is a must. This museum starts in the beginning and brings us up to the present: Wooden ships, slave ships, the first steam ship—The S.S. Savannah—to cross the Atlantic Ocean. The museum has daily tours.

Green-Meldrim House
(Bull Street between Harris and Charlton Streets)

The Green-Meldrim House was General William Tecumseh Sherman's headquarters in Savannah. This is where some believe that he met with African-Americans to determine the needs of the newly-freed slaves, and not at Second African Baptist Church. The museum has daily tours.

Civil Rights Museum
(Martin Luther King Jr. Blvd. and Taylor Street)

This is the place to find out about charge plates (plastic money) and how the Savannah boycott helped the African-Americans win integration peacefully here in Savannah. The Civil-Rights museum has daily tours.

The Roundhouse Railroad Museum
(Martin Luther King Jr. between Louisville Rd. and Harris Street)

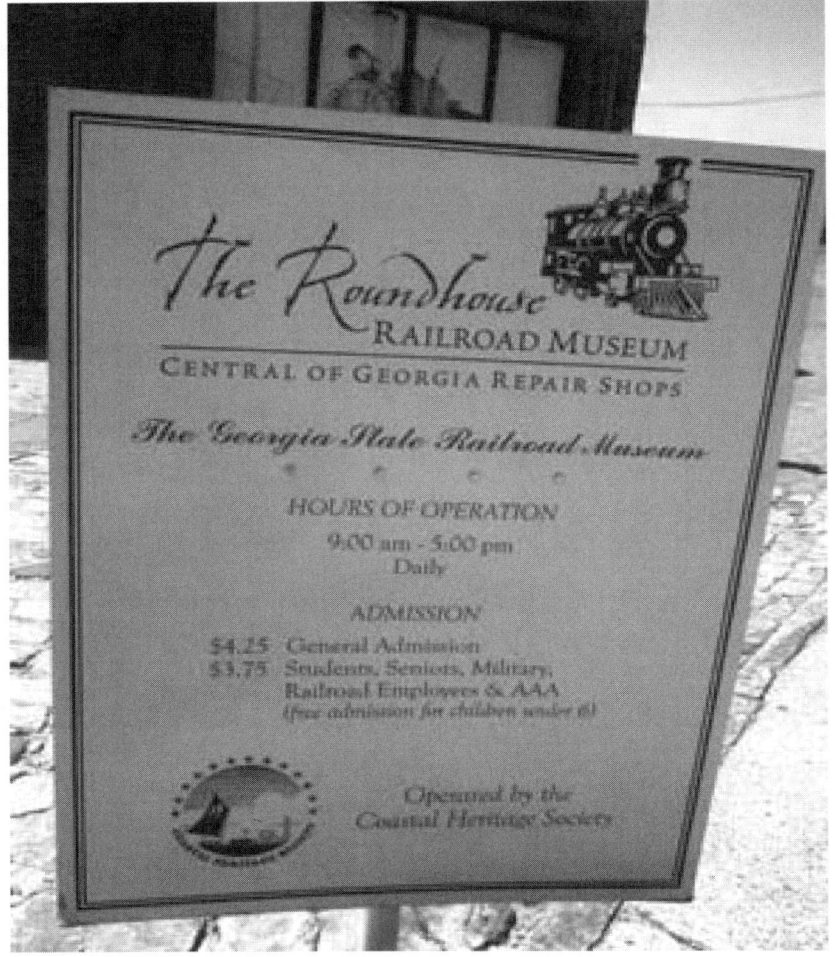

Since I was little boy, trains have always fascinated me. Visit the Roundhouse Railroad Museum. Take a ride on a train. Watch the trains on the turntable, inspect the old engines and rail cars, or watch the model trains in the buff room. The museum has daily tours.

Fort Pulaski
(On US Highway 80 East)

Fort Pulaski is hidden behind demilunes (tunnels) and an alligator-infested moat. This fort was used for many things: The Immortal 600 was imprisoned here in retaliation for Andersonville Prison. It was a stop on the Underground Railroad for run-away slaves. For Civil War buffs this is a must see. Fort Pulaski has daily tours.

Colonial Park Cemetery
(Liberty and Abercorn Streets)

Colonial Park Cemetery was Savannah's Public Burial Ground from 1753 to 1850. Probably the most famous person buried here is Button Gwinnett; however, we are not certain that he is here. A small temple was built in his honor in Colonial Park Cemetery. He is one of the three Georgia signers of the Declaration of Independence. General Lachlan McIntosh killed Button Gwinnett in a duel. McIntosh is also, buried in Colonial Park Cemetery. During daylight hours, visitors are allowed to enter Colonial Park Cemetery.

Old Fort Jackson
(1 Fort Jackson Road, follow signs off President Street Extension)

The Confederacy made Old Fort Jackson its headquarters of the Savannah River Defenses. It was the home of the Savannah River Squadron, and three ironclads operated out of Old Fort Jackson, the C.S.S. Savannah, C.S.S. Atlanta, and the C.S.S. Georgia. Old Fort Jackson did its job of protecting Savannah, until General William T. Sherman came into Savannah on December 20, 1864.

Forsyth Park

Forsyth Park is only one of Savannah's many beautiful parks. It has lush green grass for you to lie on or walk, or play on. You can let yourself go here, or show off your tennis game on the tennis courts. This park has a magnificent fountain that runs green water, in and around St. Patrick's Day, and its all done with a little elfin magic. The Confederate Soldier stands guard just south of this fountain. When in Savannah, please allow yourself some time to relax in this most beautiful of parks.

Questions You May Ask Your Next Savannah Tour Guide

1- Why did General Sherman not burn Savannah?

2- After Savannah surrendered, what was the first message sent to President Lincoln by General Sherman?

3- Why does Savannah's City Hall have a gold dome?

4- Why did many African-Americans own other African-Americans?

5- Why was General Sherman asked to leave the room when African-Americans talked with the Secretary of Defense Stanton at Second African Baptist Church?

6- Where did the word "Nigger" and "That's my Nigger", used by the rappers and younger generation of African-Americans, come from?

7- Why was slavery so successful?

8- Why is there so many churches in African-American neighborhoods?

9- Who helped the British win the battle on Bull Street at Madison Square in 1778?

10- Where in Georgia did they sell wings for African-Americans to fly back to Heaven?

11- Where in Georgia did slavery continue until 1921?

12- Who was the first white man to go to jail on the testimony of a black man in Georgia?

13-Where were the first slaves officially freed in Georgia during the Civil War?

14-Since Georgia was a no-slave colony, was General Oglethorpe against slavery?

15-The Church of Georgia questioned the morality of slavery when the colony of Georgia demanded slaves to compete with the other slave colonies. What Minister gave the answer and smoothed the way for slavery in the colony of Georgia?

16-Why are most African-Americans still having trouble closing the gap between themselves and other ethnic groups?

17-Did Savannah have any black slavers?

18-What was the name of the last slave ship to bring slaves from Africa to Georgia?

Answers

1-Savannah gave no resistance and the Central of Georgia Railroad stock manager Charles Clark Miller, disobeyed the orders of The Central of Georgia Railroad to burn everything before the Union Forces arrive.

2-General Sherman gave the City of Savannah to President Lincoln as a Christmas gift in 1864.

3-The gold dome is in recognition of Savannah being the capital of Georgia from 1782 to 1785.

4-Most African-Americans who owned other African-Americans had bought their family members out of slavery, and it was cheaper to allow other family member to remain slaves than to free them.

5-During the occupation of Savannah the Union Troops began to molest and rape African-American women, and the African-American leaders did not want to speak of this problem in front of General Sherman.

6-The word "Nigger" comes from the poor pronunciation of the word "Negro," and the phrase "That's my nigger" is what the slave owner would tell the sheriff at the jail: "That's my nigger," as he pointed out his slaves in the lock-up. So we have the rappers and young African-Americans using the same terms of the old slave masters.

7-Many Africans and African-Americans were more than happy to do whatever it took to make their slave masters happy. For example: Many African kings sold other Africans to the slave traders for two or three dollars each. The slave traders would sell the same slave for six or seven hundred dollars each in the New World. The best slave drivers were African-Americans, and the best slave catchers were also African-Americans. This cooperation is what made slavery a successful venture. Example: The Haitian Monument is in honor of the Haitians who fought on the side of the Colonists (slave owners) in the siege of Savannah in 1779. In addition, the Haitians fought along with the French who were holding their own people in bondage in Haiti, and against slaves who fought with the British hoping to win their own freedom from the Colonists.

8-During slavery, many slaves used religion to make them forget about slavery for the moment, and some slave owners even used religion to control their slaves. Many jack-leg preachers claimed to have gotten the calling to the pulpit, but trying to avoid the hot sun in the fields may have been a better explanation for their religious calling. Old habits are hard to break.

9-A slave of Governor Wright, Quamino Dolly, showed the British troops an alternate way into Savannah which gave them a huge advantage. The colony lost 577 men to only thirteen for the British.

10-During the "Christ Craze" of 1889, Jacob Orth alias DuPont Bell, was selling wings to African-Americans for five dollars a pair in Liberty County, Georgia.

11-The African-American workers that lived on the John S. Williams plantation in Jasper County were locked up every night and got no pay for their labor, nor were they allowed to leave the plantation unattended.

12-John S. Williams was convicted of murdering Lindsey Peterson and sentenced to life in prison on Clyde Manning's testimony. Manning was a black man.

13-In 1862, General David Hunter issued field order #7. This order freed all the slaves at the Fort Pulaski, in all of Georgia, South Carolina, and Florida. Almost immediately, President Lincoln rescinded General Hunter's order, but this brave move on the general's part may have helped President Lincoln issue his emancipation proclamation a year later.

14-No, true, General Oglethorpe owned no land or slaves in Georgia, but he owned much land and many slaves in South Carolina. In addition, Oglethorpe was the Deputy Governor of the Royal African Company founded in 1672 to win for England a larger share of the slave trade between West Africa and the New World.

15-Reverend George Whitefield was for slavery and the church members wanted to know how one could be for slavery and abide by a belief in the brotherhood of man? The good Reverend's response was, "The brotherhood of man only applies in Heaven."

16-Ignorance and habit are the main culprits. Ignorant people have ignorant children. Slavery taught African-Americans to think nothing of themselves. Now it is habit. We use terms like, "You're my nigger," and "That's my nigger." We seem to have forgotten that these are terms that the slave owners used during slavery.

17-Yes, Savannah had one black slaver and his name was Abraham Beasley. He married Matilda Taylor, who later became Mother Beasley.

18-The slave ship Wanderer was seized at Jekyl Island, Georgia in 1858 with 408 slaves aboard. One of the owners, Charles Lamaar, was one of the defendants declared not guilty at the Savannah Customs Clearing House, for illegally bringing these slaves into American territory. The importation of slaves had been outlawed in 1807.

Bibliography

Albu, Susan H., Duncan, John D. *Tour Guide Study Manual.* Savannah, GA. Parking Services, 1993.

Beney, Peter. *The Majesty of Savannah.* Gretna, Louisiana. Pelican Publishing Company, Inc., 1992.

Elmore, Charles J., Ph.D. "Black America Series." Savannah Georgia. Charlston, S.C. Arcadia Publishing, 2002.

Freeman, Gregory A. *Lay This Body Down.* Chicago, Illinois. Chicago Review Press, Inc., 1999.

Grant, Donald L. "The Way It Was In the South." *The Black Experience in Georgia.* Ed. Jonathan Grant. New York, N.Y. Carol Publishing Group, 1993.

Hoskins, Charles Lwanga. *Out of Yamacraw And Beyond: Discovering Black Savannah.* Savannah, G.A. Gullah Press, 2002.

McFeely, William S. *Memoirs of General William T. Sherman.* New York, N.Y. Da Capo Press, Inc., 1984.

Rogers, George A., Saunders, Frank R. Jr. *Swamp Water and Wiregrass: Historical Sketches of Coastal Georgia.* Macon, GA. Mercer University Press, 1984.

Tuck, Stephen G. N. "Beyond Atlanta." *The Struggle for Racial Equality in Georgia, 1940-1980.* Athens, Georgia. University of Georgia Press, 2001.

Index

A

Abraham Sheftall House, 123
Adams, Jr., Mayor Floyd, 55, 83
Adams, Sr., Floyd, 55
African –American Baptist Missionary, 15
African-American Monument, 19
African-American Sculptor, Jerome Meadows, 14
Air Space, Savannah first use of, 21
American Colonization Society, 57
American Missionary Association, 88, 90
Andrew Low House 118
Angelou, Maya, 18
Answers to Questions, 148-152
Armillary Sphere, 122
Arnold, Mayor Richard, 17

B

Back to Africa Movement, 12
Ballast stone, 21
Barracoons, 18
Battersby-Heritage House, 118
Battle of Monterey, 112
Battlefield Savannah Heritage Park, 39
Beach, Alfred E., 90
Beach Institute, 90, 134
Beasley, Abraham, 79, 152
Beasley, Matilda (Mother Beasley), 79
Bedrock of the African-American Baptist Church in Savannah, 52
Bench Marking General Oglethorpe's Tent Site, 29
Bethesda Orphanage, 121
Big Ben 97
Bird Girl, 78
Black Frank, 46, 47
Black Star Steamship Line, 11
Blue Angel Airplane, 67

Bonaventure Cemetery, 78
Bobbies, 83
Brampton's Barn, 15
Brampton's plantation, 33, 40, 54
Bryan, Rev. Andrew W., 15, 33, 40, 54
  Historical Marker, 14
  Grave, 54
Bryan, Joseph, 35
Bull River Yacht Club House, 68
Bull Street Library, 59
Butler, Pierce, 36
Bynes-Royall Funeral Home, 42

C

Calhoun, John C., 117
Callaway, Cab, 42
Campbell, William, 33
Cap' N Sam, 19
Carnegie Library, 84
Carr, James, 33
Carver State Bank, 44, 55, 107
Central of GA Railroad, 9, 149
Old Warehouse & Office Bldg, 10
Champion-McAlpin House, 109
Chatham County Courthouse, 37
Chatham County Jail, 38
Churches:
  Christ Church Anglican, 116
  Ethiopian Church of Jesus Christ, 15
  First African Baptist, 32, 34, 53, 54, 106, 136
  First Baptist, 114
  First Bryan Baptist, 15, 54
  First Congregational, 88, 90
  Lutheran Church of Ascension, 115
  Methodist Trinity, 110
  Second African Baptist, 54, 93, 94, 113, 126, 140

Index

St Augustine's, 46
St Johns Episcopal, 113
St Matthew's, 45, 46
St Phillip AME, 43
St Stephens's, 46, 89
Unitarian Universal (Jingle Bell Church), 89
Wesley Monumental, 117
City Hall, 29, 95
Civic Center, 38, 105
Civil Rights Museum, 41, 44, 141
Cobblestones, 21
Cochran, Lt Comdr., Donnie, 67
Cockspur Island, 23, 75
  Lighthouse, 74
Colonial Park Cemetery, 144
Colored Sign, 9, 99
Confederate Cross in Font of an African-American Grave, 52
Confederate Soldier, 146
Container Ship Entering Savannah Port, 16
Cotton Exchange, 21, 27
Courthouse Square, 131
Crawford, William Harris, 125
Crawford Square, 125
Cunningham, Rev. Henry Cox, 53
  Former Home, 93
Cupp, Robert, 22
Cuyler-Brownville Area, 55
Cuyler Street School, 46

D
Daddy Grace, 19, 47, 58, 59
Daffin Park, 62
Daffin Park's Pavilion and Fish Pond, 63
Daughters of the Confederacy, 51
Davenport House, 123, 135
Davis, Ulysses, 134
Debtor's Colony, 17
DeRenne, George, 37
Deveaux, Jane, 88
Deveaux, Col. John, 28, 88
Dolphin's Sighting, 68

Dunbar Theater, 42

E
Eichberg, Alfred, 9
Elbert, Samuel, 38
Ellis, Henry, 111
Emancipation Proclamation, 95
Excursion boats, 20

F
Factors Walk, 27
Filature House or Silk House, 120
First Volunteers of South Carolina, 77
Freedom Fighters, 77
Flame of Freedom, 37
Fonvielle, Mr., 44
Former Residence of Ralph Mark Gilbert, 57
Forrest Gump Bench, 114
Forsyth Park Fountain 146
Fort Pulaski, 72, 75, 76, 77
Fort Screven, 71, 72
Francis Bartow House, 108
Franciscan Handmaids Catholic School, 56
Franklin, Benjamin, 30, 106
Frazier, Garrison, 113
Frazier Homes, 45
Fred Wessel's Projects, 92
Free to Fly Fountain, 87
Freeman's Bureau, 90
Frog Town, 30

G
Gambling on the River, 68
Garvey, Marcus 11
General Geary, 17
George & Martha (Cannons), 28
Georgia Infirmary Historical Marker, 80
Georgia's Motto, 100
Georgia State Industrial College for Colored Youth, 65
German Memorial Fountain, 109

Index

Gibbons, George, 33
Gilbert, Rev. Ralph Mark, 41, 57, 95
Gilmore, Gen. Quincy, 77
Girl Scout Monument, 110
Glen Bill, 65
Gopher Wood Pulpit, 35
Grayson Stadium, 62
Green-Meldrim House, 94, 113, 140
Greene, Gen., Nathaniel, 126
   Monument, 116
   Square, 126
Gusman Record Shop, 83
Gwinnett, Button, 144

H
Haitians, 31
Hatian-American Historical
   Society, 31
Haitian Monument, 31
Hamilton-Turner House, 118
Hanes, Marsh, 77
Heritage place Apartments, 56
Hermitage Plantation, 10, 11
Highway 80 and the Marshes, 69
Hill, Bobby, 55
Hill Hall, 65
Hill, Walter Bernard, 65
Hunter, Gen David, 77, 151
Houston, Rev. Ulysses L., 93
Hutchinson Island, 19

I
I-16 Off and On Ramp, 48
Irish Monument, 25
Irish and Robert Emmet Park, 25

J
Jay, William, 25, 36, 114, 119
Jepson Center, 138
Johnson, Mayor, Dr. Otis, 55
Johnson, Robert, 116
Jones, Noble, 70
Jordan, Dr. Abigail, 19

K
Kennedy, Robert, 54
King Louis XIV, 28
King, Jr., Rev. Martin Luther, 57, 94, 126
King Mannah Funeral, 57
Kongo, Kosmogram, 33, 34
King-Tisdell Cottage, 87

L
La Florida, 70
Lamar, Charles, 152
Laurel Grove Cemetery, 46, 47
Laurel Grove South Cemetery
   Historical Marker, 49
Law, W. W., (Mr. Civil Rights), 49, 54, 99
Law's Burial Plot, 50
Lazaretto, 18, 73
Lee, Gen., Robert E., 75, 76
Leile, Rev. George, 15, 33, 40, 54
Levy's Department Store, 37
Liberty Boys, 38
Lincoln, Abraham President, 11, 77, 95, 98, 101
Love, Emmanuel King, 33
Low, Juliette Gordon, 97, 98

M
Maddox, Lester, 58
Madison, Pres. James, 113
Manning, Clyde, 151
Marker in Green Square, 94
Market Square, 111
Marquis de Lafayette, 25
Marshall, Rev. Andrew Cox, 31, 33, 53, Grave, 53
Massie School, 117
McCory's Lunch Counter, 37
McDonough Row Houses, 122
McKane, Dr. Alice, 56, 57
McKane, Dr. Cornelius, 57
McKinley, Pres. William, 28
McIntosh, Gen Lachlan, 144
Melody Theater, 85, 86

Index

Mercer, Johnny, 78
Mercer-Wilder House, 112
Midnight in the Garden of Good and Evil, (Book) (Movie), 79, 112, 118
Miller, Charles Clark, 149
MLK Boulevard, 17, 36, 37, 44, 58
Monroe, Pres., James 71
Morrison, Toni, 88
Mulberry Plantation, 27
Mulberry Inn, 127
Must See Places, 129-146

N
NAACP, 41, 50, 82
New Tybee Island House, 74
Norris, John, 112

O
O'Connor, Flannery, 118
Odingsells, Anthony, 77
Oglethrope, Gen. James E., 12, 13, 38, 70, 149, 151
 Monument, 12, 114
 Square, 119
Old Barnard Street School, 107
Old Charity Hospital Site, 57
Old Freight Yard, 91
Old Fort Jackson, 145
Old Harbor Light, 24
Old Jewish Education Alliance, 108
Old Negro Burial Ground, 88, 121
Old Site of Dunbar Theater, 42
Old Site of Star Theater, 43
Old Stables and Slave Quarters, 26, 133
Old Tybee Island House, 73
Old Union Station, 9, 39
Old Warehouse & Office Building of Central of Georgia Railroad, 10
Oliver Sturgess House, 120
Olmstead, Col. Charles, 76, 77
Olympic Cauldron, 23
Orth, Jacob (Dupont Bell), 151

Outcast, (Hip-Hop Group), 45
Owen-Thomas House, 26, 119, 132

P
Pink House, 120
Pitt, William (Earl of Chatham), 107
Pollard, William, 95
Porter, James, 56, 95
Porzio's Restaurant, Site of, 59
Preston, William G., 27, 115
Prince Hall, 86
Pringle, Duncan, Old Grocery Store, 84
Pulaski, Count Casimir, 75, 108
 Monument, 112

Q
Quamino Dolly, 149
Questions You May Ask Your Next Savannah Tour Guide, 148-149

R
Red Cross Building, 121
Restaurant with Separate Doors for White and Colored, 99
Reynolds, John, 120
River Street Mall, 22
Robertson, Robbie, 81, 82
Rose of Sharon Apartments, 89, 121
Roundhouse Railroad Museum, 40, 142
Royal African Company, 151
Ruins of African-American Businesses of Yesteryears, 40, 41

S
Salzburger Monument and Park, 25
Sandfly Historical Marker, 64
Savannah Beautiful Squares 103-127
Savannah-Chatham Metropolitan Police Department, 96
Savannah College of Arts and De-

Index

signs (SCAD), 10, 82, 83
Savannah Grey Bricks, 9, 11, 75
Savannah History Museum, 9
Savannah International Trade & Convention center, 22
Savannah Pharmacy, 44
Savannah Race Track, 36
Savannah State Industrial College for Colored Youth, 65
Savannah State University, 65
Savannah Theater, 114
Scarborough House, 37
Scott, Dred, 97, 98
Seaboard Coastline Railroad, 9, 91
Seaman's House, 127
Sergeant Jasper Monument, 113
Sherman, Gen. William T., 17, 93, 94, 95, 100, 113, 126, 149
Ship of the Sea Maritime Museum, 37, 139
Simms, James, 56, 100
Site of Old Georgia Infirmary, 80
Slaves Burial Marker, 51
Slave Market of Joseph Bryan, 36
Snead, Sam, 22
Sons of Liberty, 38
SS Savannah, 36, 71
St James Square, 110
St John the Baptist Cathedral, 13, 95, 96, 118, 137
St Joseph/Candler Hospital, 80
St Pius X High School, 83
Stain Glass Windows, First African Baptist Church, 33
Stanton, Edwin M., 94
Stiles, George, 46
Stranger Burial Marker, 51

T
Taft, Pres. William Howard, 66
Talmadge, Gov. Herman, 16
Talmadge Memorial Bridge, 16
Taney, Roger B., 98
Taylor, Matilda (Mother Beasley), 79, 152
Taylor, Susie King, 90
Temple Mickve Israel, 112
Telfair Family 110
Telfair Academy of Arts and Science, 110
The Landings, 61
Thomas Square, 60
Thomas, Clarence, Supreme Court Justice, 59, 83, 85
Tomochichi's Grave, 115
Toomer, Louis Burke, 55
Troup, George Michael, 122
Trustees Four Prohibitions, 12
Turner, Bishop Henry McNeal, 11, 43
Two Houses on 37th Street, 48
Tybee Island, 18, 70
Lighthouse 72, 73

U
Union Station, 9, 39
Underground Railroad, 34, 136
United House of Prayer for All People, 47
United States Custom House, 7, 28, 88

V
Victory Drive, 60, 61
Vietnam Memorial, 24
Visitor's Center, 9, 39
Viscount Percival, 115

W
Wage Earner bank, 44
Wanderer, (slave ship), 152
Warren, Gen. Joseph, 124
Washington, Pres. George, 28
Washington Gordon Monument, 115
Waving Girl, Florence Martus, 23, 75
Wayne, James Moore, 97
Wesley, Rev. John, 26
Monument, 26

Index

White Sign, 9
Whitefield, Rev. George, 151,
    Square, 121
Whitney, Eli, 27
Williams, Hosea, 37, 115
Williams, Jim, 112
Williams, John S., 151
William Seafood's Sign, 67
Williams, Thomas, 79
Witcover, Hyman, 29
Wormsloe Fountain, 123
Wormsloe Plantation, 63, 64, 70
Wright, James, 115
Wright, Sr. Richard R., 65

Y

Yamacraw Villiage, 13, 30
Yamacraw Village Square, 14
Young, Andrew, 56